D0805269

MOBY-DICK

Herman Melville

SPARK PUBLISHING

Spark Publishing
A Division of Barnes & Noble
120 Fifth Avenue
New York, NY 10011
www.sparknotes.com

ISBN-13: 978-1-4114-0710-7
ISBN-10: 1-4114-0710-5

Please submit changes or report errors to www.sparknotes.com/errors.

Printed in the United States.

10 9 8 7 6 5 4 3 2 1

Contents

CONTEXT

ERMAN MELVILLE WAS BORN in New York City in 1819, the third of eight children born to Maria Gansevoort Melville and Allan Melville, a prosperous importer of foreign goods. When the family business failed at the end of the 1820s, the Melvilles relocated to Albany in an attempt to revive their fortunes. A string of further bad luck and overwork, however, drove his father to an early grave, and the young Melville was forced to start working in a bank at the age of thirteen.

After a few more years of formal education, Melville left school at eighteen to become an elementary school teacher. This career was abruptly cut short and followed by a brief tenure as a newspaper reporter. Running out of alternatives on land, Melville made his first sea voyage at nineteen, as a merchant sailor on a ship bound for Liverpool, England. He returned to America the next summer to seek his fortune in the West. After settling briefly in Illinois, he went back east in the face of continuing financial difficulties.

Finally, driven to desperation at twenty-one, Melville committed to a whaling voyage of indefinite destination and scale on board a ship called the *Acushnet*. This journey took him around the continent of South America, across the Pacific Ocean, and to the South Seas, where he abandoned ship with a fellow sailor in the summer of 1842, eighteen months after setting out from New York. The two men found themselves in the Marquesas Islands, where they accidentally wandered into the company of a tribe of cannibals. Lamed with a bad leg, Melville became separated from his companion and spent a month alone in the company of the natives. This experience later formed the core of his first novel, *Typee: A Peep at Polynesian Life,* published in 1846. An indeterminate mixture of fact and fiction, Melville's fanciful travel narrative remained the most popular and successful of his works during his lifetime.

Life among these natives and other exotic experiences abroad provided Melville with endless literary conceits. Armed with the voluminous knowledge obtained from constant reading while at sea, Melville wrote a series of novels detailing his adventures and his philosophy of life. *Typee* was followed by *Omoo* (1847) and *Mardi and a Voyage Thither* (1849), two more novels about his Polynesian

CHARACTER LIST

Ishmael   The narrator, and a junior member of the crew of the *Pequod*. Ishmael doesn't play a major role in the events of the novel, but much of the narrative is taken up by his eloquent, verbose, and extravagant discourse on whales and whaling.

Ahab   The egomaniacal captain of the *Pequod*. Ahab lost his leg to Moby Dick. He is single-minded in his pursuit of the whale, using a mixture of charisma and terror to persuade his crew to join him. As a captain, he is dictatorial but not unfair. At moments he shows a compassionate side, caring for the insane Pip and musing on his wife and child back in Nantucket.

Moby Dick   The great white sperm whale. Moby Dick, also referred to as the White Whale, is an infamous and dangerous threat to seamen, considered by Ahab the incarnation of evil and a fated nemesis.

Starbuck   The first mate of the *Pequod*. Starbuck questions Ahab's judgment, first in private and later in public. He is a Quaker who believes that Christianity offers a way to interpret the world around him, although he is not dogmatic or pushy about his beliefs. Starbuck acts as a conservative force against Ahab's mania.

Queequeg   Starbuck's skilled harpooner and Ishmael's best friend. Queequeg was once a prince from a South Sea island who stowed away on a whaling ship in search of adventure. He is a composite of elements of African, Polynesian, Islamic, Christian, and Native American cultures. He is brave and generous, and enables Ishmael to see that race has no bearing on a man's character.

Stubb   The second mate of the *Pequod*. Stubb, chiefly characterized by his mischievous good humor, is easygoing and popular. He proves a bit of a nihilist, always trusting in fate and refusing to assign too much significance to anything.

Tashtego   Stubb's harpooner, Tashtego is a Gay Head Indian from Martha's Vineyard, one of the last of a tribe about to disappear. Tashtego performs many of the skilled tasks aboard the ship, such as tapping the case of spermaceti in the whale's head. Like Queequeg, Tashtego embodies certain characteristics of the "noble savage" and is meant to defy racial stereotypes. He is, however, more practical and less intellectual than Queequeg: like many a common sailor, Tashtego craves rum.

Flask   A native of Tisbury on Martha's Vineyard and the third mate of the *Pequod*. Short and stocky, Flask has a confrontational attitude and no reverence for anything. His stature has earned him the nickname "King-Post," because he resembles a certain type of short, square timber.

Daggoo   Flask's harpooner. Daggoo is a physically enormous, imperious-looking African. Like Queequeg, he stowed away on a whaling ship that stopped near his home. Daggoo is less prominent in the narrative than either Queequeg or Tashtego.

Pip   A young black boy who fills the role of a cabin boy or jester on the *Pequod*. Pip has a minimal role in the beginning of the narrative but becomes important when he goes insane after being left to drift alone in the sea for some time. Like the fools in Shakespeare's plays, he is half idiot and half prophet, often perceiving things that others don't.

Fedallah   A strange, "oriental" old Parsee (Persian fire-worshipper) whom Ahab has brought on board unbeknownst to most of the crew. Fedallah has a very striking appearance: around his head is a turban made from his own hair, and he wears a black Chinese jacket and pants. He is an almost supernaturally skilled hunter and also serves as a prophet to Ahab. Fedallah keeps his distance from the rest of the crew, who for their part view him with unease.

Peleg   A well-to-do retired whaleman of Nantucket and a Quaker. As one of the principal owners of the *Pequod*, Peleg, along with Captain Bildad, takes care of hiring the crew. When the two are negotiating wages for Ishmael and Queequeg, Peleg plays the generous one, although his salary offer is not terribly impressive.

Bildad   Another well-to-do Quaker ex-whaleman from Nantucket who owns a large share of the *Pequod*. Bildad is (or pretends to be) crustier than Peleg in negotiations over wages. Both men display a business sense and a bloodthirstiness unusual for Quakers, who are normally pacifists.

Father Mapple A former whaleman and now the preacher in the New Bedford Whaleman's Chapel. Father Mapple delivers a sermon on Jonah and the whale in which he uses the Bible to address the whalemen's lives. Learned but also experienced, he is an example of someone whose trials have led him toward God rather than bitterness or revenge.

Captain Boomer The jovial captain of the English whaling ship the *Samuel Enderby*. Boomer lost his arm in an accident involving Moby Dick. Unlike Ahab, Boomer is glad to have escaped with his life, and he sees further pursuit of the whale as madness. He is a foil for Ahab, as the two men react in different ways to a similar experience.

Gabriel   A sailor aboard the *Jeroboam*. Part of a Shaker
             sect, Gabriel has prophesied that Moby Dick is the
             incarnation of the Shaker god and that any attempts
             to harm him will result in disaster. His prophecies
             have been borne out by the death of the *Jeroboam*'s
             mate in a whale hunt and the plague that rages aboard
             the ship.

ANALYSIS OF MAJOR CHARACTERS

ISHMAEL

Despite his centrality to the story, Ishmael doesn't reveal much about himself to the reader. We know that he has gone to sea out of some deep spiritual malaise and that shipping aboard a whaler is his version of committing suicide—he believes that men aboard a whaling ship are lost to the world. It is apparent from Ishmael's frequent digressions on a wide range of subjects—from art, geology, and anatomy to legal codes and literature—that he is intelligent and well educated, yet he claims that a whaling ship has been "[his] Yale College and [his] Harvard." He seems to be a self-taught Renaissance man, good at everything but committed to nothing. Given the mythic, romantic aspects of *Moby-Dick*, it is perhaps fitting that its narrator should be an enigma: not everything in a story so dependent on fate and the seemingly supernatural needs to make perfect sense.

Additionally, Ishmael represents the fundamental contradiction between the story of *Moby-Dick* and its setting. Melville has created a profound and philosophically complicated tale and set it in a world of largely uneducated working-class men; Ishmael, thus, seems less a real character than an instrument of the author. No one else aboard the *Pequod* possesses the proper combination of intellect and experience to tell this story. Indeed, at times even Ishmael fails Melville's purposes, and he disappears from the story for long stretches, replaced by dramatic dialogues and soliloquies from Ahab and other characters.

AHAB

Ahab, the *Pequod*'s obsessed captain, represents both an ancient and a quintessentially modern type of hero. Like the heroes of Greek or Shakespearean tragedy, Ahab suffers from a single fatal flaw, one he shares with such legendary characters as Oedipus and Faust. His tremendous overconfidence, or hubris, leads him to defy common sense and believe that, like a god, he can enact his will and remain immune to the forces of nature. He considers Moby Dick the embodiment of evil in the world, and he pursues the White Whale monomaniacally because he believes it his inescapable fate to destroy this evil. According to the critic M. H. Abrams, such a tragic hero "moves us to pity because, since he is not an evil man, his misfortune is greater than he deserves; but he moves us also to fear, because we recognize similar possibilities of error in our own lesser and fallible selves."

Unlike the heroes of older tragic works, however, Ahab suffers from a fatal flaw that is not necessarily inborn but instead stems from damage, in his case both psychological and physical, inflicted by life in a harsh world. He is as much a victim as he is an aggressor, and the symbolic opposition that he constructs between himself and Moby Dick propels him toward what he considers a destined end.

MOBY DICK

In a sense, Moby Dick is not a character, as the reader has no access to the White Whale's thoughts, feelings, or intentions. Instead, Moby Dick is an impersonal force, one that many critics have interpreted as an allegorical representation of God, an inscrutable and all-powerful being that humankind can neither understand nor defy. Moby Dick thwarts free will and cannot be defeated, only accommodated or avoided. Ishmael tries a plethora of approaches to describe whales in general, but none proves adequate. Indeed, as Ishmael points out, the majority of a whale is hidden from view at all times. In this way, a whale mirrors its environment. Like the whale, only the surface of the ocean is available for human observation and interpretation, while its depths conceal unknown and unknowable truths. Furthermore, even when Ishmael does get his hands on a "whole" whale, he is unable to determine which part— the skeleton, the head, the skin—offers the best understanding of the whole living, breathing creature; he cannot localize the essence of the whale. This conundrum can be read as a metaphor for the human relationship with the Christian God (or any other god, for that matter): God is unknowable and cannot be pinned down.

STARBUCK, STUBB, AND FLASK

The *Pequod*'s three mates are used primarily to provide philosophical contrasts with Ahab. Starbuck, the first mate, is a religious man. Sober and conservative, he relies on his Christian faith to determine his actions and interpretations of events. Stubb, the second mate, is jolly and cool in moments of crisis. He has worked in the dangerous occupation of whaling for so long that the possibility of death has ceased to concern him. A fatalist, he believes that things happen as they are meant to and that there is little that he can do about it. Flask simply enjoys the thrill of the hunt and takes pride in killing whales. He doesn't stop to consider consequences at all and is "utterly lost . . . to all sense of reverence" for the whale. All three of these perspectives are used to accentuate Ahab's monomania. Ahab reads his experiences as the result of a conspiracy against him by some larger force. Unlike Flask, he thinks and interprets. Unlike Stubb, he believes that he can alter his world. Unlike Starbuck, he places himself rather than some external set of principles at the center of the cosmic order that he discerns.

THEMES, MOTIFS & SYMBOLS

THEMES

Themes are the fundamental and often universal ideas explored in a literary work.

THE LIMITS OF KNOWLEDGE

As Ishmael tries, in the opening pages of *Moby-Dick*, to offer a simple collection of literary excerpts mentioning whales, he discovers that, throughout history, the whale has taken on an incredible multiplicity of meanings. Over the course of the novel, he makes use of nearly every discipline known to man in his attempts to understand the essential nature of the whale. Each of these systems of knowledge, however, including art, taxonomy, and phrenology, fails to give an adequate account. The multiplicity of approaches that Ishmael takes, coupled with his compulsive need to assert his authority as a narrator and the frequent references to the limits of observation (men cannot see the depths of the ocean, for example), suggest that human knowledge is always limited and insufficient. When it comes to Moby Dick himself, this limitation takes on allegorical significance. The ways of Moby Dick, like those of the Christian God, are unknowable to man, and thus trying to interpret them, as Ahab does, is inevitably futile and often fatal.

THE DECEPTIVENESS OF FATE

In addition to highlighting many portentous or foreshadowing events, Ishmael's narrative contains many references to fate, creating the impression that the *Pequod*'s doom is inevitable. Many of the sailors believe in prophecies, and some even claim the ability to foretell the future. A number of things suggest, however, that characters are actually deluding themselves when they think that they see the work of fate and that fate either doesn't exist or is one of the many forces about which human beings can have no distinct knowledge. Ahab, for example, clearly exploits the sailors' belief in fate to manipulate them into thinking that the quest for Moby Dick is their common destiny. Moreover, the prophesies of Fedallah and others seem to be undercut in Chapter 99, when various individuals interpret the doubloon in different ways, demonstrating that humans project what they want to see when they try to interpret signs and portents.

The Exploitative Nature of Whaling

At first glance, the *Pequod* seems like an island of equality and fellowship in the midst of a racist, hierarchically structured world. The ship's crew includes men from all corners of the globe and all races who seem to get along harmoniously. Ishmael is initially uneasy upon meeting Queequeg, but he quickly realizes that it is better to have a "sober cannibal than a drunken Christian" for a shipmate. Additionally, the conditions of work aboard the *Pequod* promote a certain kind of egalitarianism, since men are promoted and paid according to their skill. However, the work of whaling parallels the other exploitative activities—buffalo hunting, gold mining, unfair trade with indigenous peoples—that characterize American and European territorial expansion. Each of the *Pequod*'s mates, who are white, is entirely dependent on a nonwhite harpooner, and nonwhites perform most of the dirty or dangerous jobs aboard the ship. Flask actually stands on Daggoo, his African harpooner, in order to beat the other mates to a prize whale. Ahab is depicted as walking over the black youth Pip, who listens to Ahab's pacing from below deck, and is thus reminded that his value as a slave is less than the value of a whale.

MOTIFS

Motifs are recurring structures, contrasts, and literary devices that can help to develop and inform the text's major themes.

Whiteness

Whiteness, to Ishmael, is horrible because it represents the unnatural and threatening: albinos, creatures that live in extreme and inhospitable environments, waves breaking against rocks. These examples reverse the traditional association of whiteness with purity. Whiteness conveys both a lack of meaning and an unreadable excess of meaning that confounds individuals. Moby Dick is the pinnacle of whiteness, and Melville's characters cannot objectively understand the White Whale. Ahab, for instance, believes that Moby Dick represents evil, while Ishmael fails in his attempts to determine scientifically the whale's fundamental nature.

SURFACES AND DEPTHS

Ishmael frequently bemoans the impossibility of examining any-thing in its entirety, noting that only the surfaces of objects and en-vironments are available to the human observer. On a live whale, for example, only the outer layer presents itself; on a dead whale, it is impossible to determine what constitutes the whale's skin, or which part—skeleton, blubber, head—offers the best understanding of the entire animal. Moreover, as the whale swims, it hides much of its body underwater, away from the human gaze, and no one knows where it goes or what it does. The sea itself is the greatest frustration in this regard: its depths are mysterious and inaccessible to Ishmael. This motif represents the larger problem of the limitations of human knowledge. Humankind is not all-seeing; we can only observe, and thus only acquire knowledge about, that fraction of entities—both individuals and environments—to which we have access: surfaces.

SYMBOLS

> *Symbols are objects, characters, figures, and colors used to represent abstract ideas or concepts.*

THE PEQUOD

Named after a Native American tribe in Massachusetts that did not long survive the arrival of white men and thus memorializing an extinction, the *Pequod* is a symbol of doom. It is painted a gloomy black and covered in whale teeth and bones, literally bristling with the mementos of violent death. It is, in fact, marked for death. Adorned like a primitive coffin, the *Pequod* becomes one.

MOBY DICK

Moby Dick possesses various symbolic meanings for various in-dividuals. To the *Pequod*'s crew, the legendary White Whale is a concept onto which they can displace their anxieties about their dangerous and often very frightening jobs. Because they have no delusions about Moby Dick acting malevolently toward men or lit-erally embodying evil, tales about the whale allow them to confront their fear, manage it, and continue to function. Ahab, on the other hand, believes that Moby Dick is a manifestation of all that is wrong with the world, and he feels that it is his destiny to eradicate this symbolic evil.

Moby Dick also bears out interpretations not tied down to spe-cific characters. In its inscrutable silence and mysterious habits, for

God gives humans the power to apprehend truth, and that men and women should be so confident in their vision of this truth as to defy any opposition. Throughout Ishmael's narrative, these two interpretations of human understanding vie with one another for primacy.

The comical process by which Ishmael befriends Queequeg introduces one of the novel's major facets: the topic of race relations. By developing a relationship with this "savage," Ishmael shows that he isn't bound by his prejudices. Indeed, his interactions with Queequeg make Ishmael realize that although most would call Queequeg a savage, the harpooner actually has a deeper understanding of what "civilization" means than most whites do, as his grooming habits demonstrate. Realizing that Queequeg treats him "with so much civility and consideration" while he himself was "guilty of great rudeness," Ishmael reexamines stereotypes about so-called savages. In fact, "for all his tattooings," says Ishmael, Queequeg "was on the whole a clean, comely looking cannibal." Queequeg's tattoos and supposed cannibalism mark him, in terms of nineteenth-century beliefs, as the ultimate savage. Tattooing is a voluntary alteration of the body that, unlike a hairstyle or clothing choice, is permanent; cannibalism is another fundamental Western taboo. Beyond these two characteristics, Queequeg is a veritable melting pot of different racial and ethnic traits: African, Polynesian, Islamic, Christian, and Native American. Allegedly from Kokovoko, an island in the South Seas, he worships an idol that looks like "a three days' old Congo baby" (West African) in a Ramadan (Islamic) ceremony and carries a tomahawk pipe (North American indigenous tribal).

CHAPTERS 10–21

CHAPTER 10: A BOSOM FRIEND

Thus, then, in our hearts' honeymoon, lay I and Queequeg—a cosy, loving pair.
(See QUOTATIONS, *p. 74)*

Contemplating Queequeg's serene comportment, Ishmael develops a great respect for his new friend, noting that "[y]ou cannot hide the soul" under tattoos and appearances. Although Ishmael still thinks of Queequeg as a savage, the latter becomes, in Ishmael's mind, "George Washington cannibalistically developed." Ishmael makes some small gestures of friendship toward Queequeg, and the two become friendly. He admires Queequeg's sincerity and lack of Christian "hollow courtesies." According to the customs of Queequeg's home, he and Queequeg are "married" after a social smoke out of the tomahawk pipe. Queequeg gives Ishmael half his belongings, and the two continue to share a bed, having many long chats. Ishmael even consents to join in Queequeg's idol worship, explaining to his Christian readers that he is only obeying the Golden Rule, as he would hope the "savage" to join in Christian worship with him.

CHAPTER 11: NIGHTGOWN
Queequeg and Ishmael awaken in the middle of the night. It is cold and the warmth of the bed and of their companionship is pleasant. They share a smoke, and Queequeg begins to recount his life story.

CHAPTER 12: BIOGRAPHICAL
Queequeg is a native of a South Pacific island called Kokovoko, which is "not down on any map; true places never are." The king's son, he desired to leave the island to see the world and, he claims, to learn about Christianity. When a whaling ship stopped at Kokovoko, he sought passage but was denied a job. He stowed away on the departing ship and, through sheer persistence, was finally taken on as a whaler. He has since become a skilled harpooner. Although his father is probably dead by now, meaning that Queequeg would be king, he can never go back, because his interaction with Christianity has made him unfit to ascend his homeland's "pure and undefiled throne." For Queequeg, Ishmael notes, "that barbed iron [Queequeg's harpoon] was in lieu of a scepter now." The two plan to go to Nantucket to find a berth aboard a whaler.

CHAPTER 13: WHEELBARROW
Together, Ishmael and Queequeg set off for Nantucket with a wheelbarrow full of their things. The people of New Bedford stare at this white man and "savage" behaving so friendly with each other. Queequeg tells Ishmael stories about the first time that he used a wheelbarrow (he picked it up instead of wheeling it) and about a white captain who attended a wedding feast on Kokovoko and made a fool of himself. On the ferry to Nantucket, a bumpkin mimics Queequeg. Queequeg flips the man around in the air to rebuke him and is subsequently scolded by the captain. A moment later, a rope in the ferry's rigging breaks, and the bumpkin is swept overboard as the ferry goes out of control. Queequeg takes charge of the ropes to secure the ferry and then dives into the water to save the man who has gone overboard, which wins everyone's respect.

CHAPTER 14: NANTUCKET

Ishmael digresses from the story to discuss the island of Nantucket. He details some of the legends about its founding and some of the tall tales that are told about life on the island. He notes that a Nantucketer "owns" the seas and that this "empire," covering two-thirds of the globe, is larger than that of any country.

CHAPTER 15: CHOWDER

Ishmael and Queequeg settle at the Try-Pots for the night, an inn owned by the cousin of the Spouter-Inn's owner. Ishmael is disturbed by an old topmast above the inn that looks ominously like a gallows. Everything on Nantucket is touched by the sea: the milk tastes of fish, and the innkeeper's wife wears a necklace of fish vertebrae. The two friends have a supper of hearty chowder.

CHAPTER 16: THE SHIP

Charged by Yojo, Queequeg's wooden idol, to seek a ship for the two men, Ishmael lights upon the *Pequod,* a ship "with an old fashioned claw-footed look about her" and "apparelled like any barbaric Ethiopian emperor, his neck heavy with pendants of polished ivory." Ishmael also calls the *Pequod* a "cannibal of a craft" because it is bejeweled with whale parts. On board, he makes a deal with Peleg and Bildad, the ship's Quaker owners, who are characterized as conniving cheapskates and bitter taskmasters. Although Quakers are generally pacifists, these two have dedicated their life to the bloody slaughter of whales. Evaluating what lay Ishmael should receive (his portion of the ship's profits and his only wages), Peleg finally gives him the 300th lay. At this time, Ishmael also learns that the ship's captain is the mysterious Ahab, named after a wicked biblical king. Although Ahab has been moody and secretive since losing his leg in an encounter with the great white whale Moby Dick, Bildad and Peleg believe in his competence and they believe him harmless, since he has a young wife and an infant child waiting for him at home.

CHAPTER 17: THE RAMADAN

Returning to the inn, Ishmael allows Queequeg a day for his "Ramadan" ceremonies and then worries when his friend doesn't answer the door in the evening. When the panicky Ishmael finally gets the door open, he finds Queequeg deep in meditation. Queequeg is unresponsive and continues to meditate until the next morning. Ishmael talks to Queequeg about the discomforts of Queequeg's religion. The next day, after a large breakfast, they return to the *Pequod.*

Chapter 18: His Mark

Though the owners object at first to his paganism, Queequeg impresses them with his skill by hitting a tiny spot of tar on the water with a harpoon. They give him the ninetieth lay, "more than ever was given a harpooneer yet out of Nantucket." Bildad tries to convert Queequeg to Christianity, but Peleg tells him to give up: "Pious harpooneers never make good voyagers—it takes the shark out of 'em; no harpooneer is worth a straw who ain't pretty sharkish." Peleg reminds Bildad that, at sea, practical concerns shove religious matters aside.

Chapter 19: The Prophet

Just after signing the papers, Ishmael and Queequeg run into a scarred and deformed man named Elijah, a prophet or perhaps merely a frightening stranger, who hints to them about the peril of signing aboard Ahab's ship. He drops references to several frightening incidents involving Ahab, but Ishmael and Queequeg disregard the man's warnings.

Chapter 20: All Astir

Over the course of several days, the ship is provisioned for the coming voyage. Ishmael hears that Ahab's health is improving—he is still recovering from the loss of his leg—but he and Queequeg have yet to meet the mysterious captain.

Chapter 21: Going Aboard

Approaching the *Pequod* at dawn, Ishmael thinks that he sees sailors boarding the ship and decides that the ship must be leaving at sunrise. Ishmael and Queequeg encounter Elijah again just before they board. Elijah asks Ishmael whether he saw "anything looking like men" boarding the ship; Ishmael replies that he did. The ship, however, is quiet save one old sailor, who informs them that the captain is already aboard. As the sun rises, the *Pequod*'s crew arrives and the ship prepares to sail.

Analysis: Chapters 10–21

In these chapters, a remarkably intense bond develops between Ishmael and Queequeg. Ishmael progresses from seeing Queequeg as a thing "hideously marred" about the face and body with tattoos to comparing Queequeg to George Washington. The two become "a cosy, loving pair" and exemplify an ideal friendship based on respect and sharing. The citizens of New Bedford, though used to seeing cannibals in their streets, are shocked by the pair's closeness, and many of Ishmael's comments about Queequeg are calculated to shock the nineteenth-century reader. Ishmael's blithe acceptance and even embracing of Queequeg's idolatry is a prime example of Melville's attempt to provoke a reaction. Though he acknowledges that he is a Presbyterian, Ishmael refuses to insist on the correctness of his own religion, instead focusing on the unity of religions and the brotherhood of man.

Ishmael's narrative continues to cast doubt on prejudice and dogma, both racial and religious. Ironically, Queequeg views his exposure to Christians as a contaminant that makes him unfit to rule his native people rather than a benefit or deliverance from ignorance. He disproves the prejudice of the Nantucket ferry's passengers and captain by saving the ferry and the bumpkin who goes overboard, demonstrating that he is not a dangerous "devil." His skill with a harpoon persuades Peleg and Bildad to ignore his religious practices and give him a berth on the *Pequod*. Though a Quaker, Peleg admits that religious principles are of little use at sea, where daring and attention to the tasks at hand are necessary for survival. There are limits, however, to Ishmael's tolerance. Queequeg's extreme abstinence during his "Ramadan" ritual provokes Ishmael to remonstrate with him—to no avail—about the folly of religious "dyspepsia," referring to the malnourishment that he believes results from fasting.

These chapters are filled with foreshadowing and dark imagery. Elijah, who shares his name with the Old Testament prophet who foretold destruction to the biblical Ahab, tells Ishmael and Queequeg that the *Pequod* is doomed. Indeed, the ship itself is an emblem of death. Named after a tribe of New England Indians killed off by white settlers, it is covered in whale bones and teeth and cloaked in dark paint. Elijah's fears seem to have some basis in fact, as he refers to incidents of bad judgment and unnecessary risk involving Ahab. Ahab himself, "desperate moody, and savage," inspires sympathy, pity, and "a strange awe" in Ishmael. Named for the Israelite king who angers God with his worship of idols, Ahab seems an ominous figure. His obsession with the whale—a sort of perverse worship—has already injured him corporeally and spiritually, and we sense that the conflict will only heighten.

CHAPTERS 22–31

CHAPTER 22: MERRY CHRISTMAS
The *Pequod* leaves Nantucket on a cold Christmas Day. Bildad and Peleg pilot the ship out of port. Ahab still has not appeared on deck. Ishmael finds the start of the voyage disconcerting and is meditating upon his situation when he receives a kick and a scolding from Peleg. The *Pequod* is soon clear of the harbor and into the open ocean, and Bildad and Peleg take a small boat back to shore as the whaling ship "plunge[s] like fate into the lone Atlantic."

CHAPTER 23: THE LEE SHORE
Ishmael offers a brief portrait of Bulkington, a sailor whom he first meets in New Bedford. Ishmael watches Bulkington steer the *Pequod* and thinks of him as a restless pioneer, fated to die at sea. Ishmael considers this kind of death infinitely preferable to fading away through cowardice, and, in an imaginary address to Bulkington, declares that the death at sea will transform Bulkington into a god.

CHAPTER 24: THE ADVOCATE
Ishmael proceeds to stand up for the whaling profession, arguing that whaling is heroic, economically critical, and has expanded geographical knowledge. He defends the dignity of whaling by pointing to the involvement of noble families in the industry, to the fact that the Bible and other books mention whales, and to the fact that Cetus, the whale, is a constellation in the southern sky. Ishmael closes by declaring that anything worthwhile that he might accomplish can be credited to his time spent on a whaling ship, his "Yale College" and his "Harvard."

CHAPTER 25: POSTSCRIPT
Ishmael adds some speculation to the previous chapter's "facts." He reminds the reader that sperm whale oil is used in the coronation of royalty, and suggests that sperm oil has been used to anoint kings because it is the best, purest, and sweetest of oils.

CHAPTER 26: KNIGHTS AND SQUIRES
In the first of the two chapters called "Knights and Squires," we meet the first mate, Starbuck, a pragmatic, reliable Nantucketer. Starbuck believes that it is rational—and necessary—to fear whales, and his reverence for nature inclines him toward superstition. He is characterized by the other officers of the *Pequod* as "careful,"

although this term is relative when used to describe a whaler. Speaking about Starbuck leads Ishmael to reflect upon the dignity of the working man. Ishmael finds evidence of God in even the "meanest mariners" and admits that he will frequently ignore people's faults to emphasize their "democratic dignity."

Chapter 27: Knights and Squires

This chapter introduces the rest of the *Pequod*'s officers. The pipe-smoking second mate, Stubb, a native of Cape Cod, is always cool under pressure and possesses "impious good humor." The third mate, Flask, a native of Tisbury on Martha's Vineyard, is a short, stocky fellow with a confrontational attitude and no reverence for the dignity of the whale. He is nicknamed "King-Post" because he resembles the short, square timber known by that name in Arctic whalers. Each mate commands one of the small harpoon boats that are sent out after whales, and each has a "squire," his harpooner: Queequeg is Starbuck's harpooner; Tashtego, "an unmixed Indian from Gay Head," on Martha's Vineyard, is Stubb's harpooner; and Daggoo, "a gigantic, coal-black negro-savage" from Africa with an imperial bearing, is Flask's harpooner.

Ishmael notes that few whalers are American-born except the officers, who are almost always American: "the native American liberally provides the brains, the rest of the world as generously supplies the muscles." The rest of the crew is also international. But, says Ishmael, all of these "Isolatoes" are "federated along one keel" and unified by their comradeship at sea and shared danger. Ishmael also mentions Pip, a poor black boy from Alabama who beats a tambourine on ship.

Chapter 28: Ahab

As the *Pequod* ranges further south and the weather improves, Ahab finally appears on deck. Ishmael observes him closely. Ahab appears a strong, willful figure, though his encounter with Moby Dick has scarred him both physically and mentally. In addition to missing a leg, Ahab is marked with a white scar down one side of his face that looks like a lightning strike. Rumor has it that the scar suddenly appeared during some "elemental strife at sea." Ahab stands watch with his false leg, carved from a whale's jaw, set into a hole bored into the deck.

CHAPTER 29: ENTER AHAB; TO HIM, STUBB

Ahab does indeed seem psychologically troubled. He maintains a total dictatorship on board. He is restless and paces the deck, and the striking of his peg leg on the wood echoes throughout the ship. When Stubb complains about Ahab's pacing, Ahab calls him a dog and advances on him. Stubb retreats. This chapter is short and dramatic, as the stage-direction title implies.

CHAPTER 30: THE PIPE

Ahab realizes that smoking no longer soothes him and that the sereneness of the activity doesn't suit his agitated, willful state of mind. He hurls his pipe overboard and resumes pacing the ship deck.

CHAPTER 31: QUEEN MAB

The next morning, Stubb tells Flask that he dreamed that Ahab kicked him with his ivory leg. An old merman in the dream points out the futility of struggling against Ahab and suggests that it may even be an honor to be kicked by such a man. (The title of this chapter, "Queen Mab," refers to Shakespeare's tragedy *Romeo and Juliet,* in which Mercutio explains how Queen Mab, a fairy, brings dreams to sleepers.) As Stubb finishes telling of his dream, Ahab shouts at the crew to be on the lookout for whales. The *Pequod*'s work has begun.

ANALYSIS: CHAPTERS 22–31

These chapters introduce the other men aboard the ship and begin to describe the onboard dynamics. The disparate nature of the crew, composed of men from various nations, doesn't prevent the ship from functioning properly. The sense of harmony on the *Pequod* is quite different from the racially divided nineteenth-century American society on land. The leadership structure of the ship is, however, divided by color: the officers are white and the sailors are from the South Sea Islands, Gay Head, Africa, and other far corners of the globe. Ishmael's offhand remark that Americans provide the "brains" and the rest of the world the "muscle" for this undertaking and many others reveals his belief in the harmony of such an arrangement.

Critic Alan Heimert has suggested that the pairing of mates and harpooners mirrors relationships of oppression in the nineteenth century. Starbuck represents New England and, just as this region depends on the Chinese/South Sea trade, he depends on Queequeg. Stubb represents the American West, and his power derives from his subordination of the Native American Indian, Tashtego. Flask represents the South and both controls and depends upon the African, Daggoo. While these pairings do reflect larger social structures, however, they also involve relationships that are much more complicated and much more interdependent than simple master-slave or boss-worker exchanges. The *Pequod* depends on cooperation for success in catching whales and sometimes for mere survival at sea, and men, in the end, are assessed according to their skill rather than race. Melville explores the development of an alternative, more egalitarian social system aboard the ship throughout *Moby-Dick*.

At this point, the irresistibly charismatic Ahab rules the ship. "[M]oody stricken Ahab [stands] before [his crew] with a crucifixion in his face"; he clearly represents a force that will not be denied. Obedience is crucial to maintaining onboard discipline and the chain of command, and captains were allowed and even expected to be tyrants. The suggestion, in Stubb's dream, that one should consider it a privilege to be abused by Ahab rationalizes his despotism and hints at the grandiose folly in which the sailors will soon become entangled.

These chapters illustrate Ishmael's peculiar style of narration. The chronological, plot-driven story is interwoven with digressions, character sketches, and rhetorical exercises. Some chapters, like Chapter 29, are presented as if they were scenes in a play. Ishmael is also given to foreboding language and foreshadowing: the *Pequod* "plunge[s] like fate," Ahab has a "crucifixion in his face," and Stubb speaks of something strange going on in the hold. The events that unfold are meant to seem like the fulfillment of Ahab's destiny and the natural consequence of his megalomaniacal behavior. Ishmael constructs his narrative to suggest and anticipate what will happen rather than to create the effect of surprise.

CHAPTERS 32–40

CHAPTER 32: CETOLOGY

"Cetology," as Ishmael explains, is "the science of whales." In this and subsequent science-centered chapters in the book, Ishmael attempts to classify whales scientifically. He includes quotations from various writings on the whale, adding that others might be able to revise this draft of a classification system. Rather than using the Linnaean classifications of family, genus, and species—which were already the standard in Melville's time—Ishmael divides whales into different "chapters" of three distinct "books": the Folio, Octavo, and Duodecimo.

CHAPTER 33: THE SPECKSYNDER

"The Specksynder" resembles the previous chapter, but it analyzes the whaling industry rather than whales. Beginning with trivia about the changing role of the specksynder (literally, "fat-cutter"), who used to be chief harpooner and captain, Ishmael moves on to a discussion of onboard leadership styles. He notes that the dependence of whalers upon one another for successful hunting and therefore wages begets its own discipline, and that a whaling ship is less hierarchical than other vessels. Nevertheless, many captains make a great show of their rank. Ahab doesn't flaunt his superiority, although he can be a tyrant. In fact, Ishmael admits that it can be hard to see exactly what is remarkable about Ahab: one must "dive . . . for [it] in the deep."

CHAPTER 34: THE CABIN-TABLE

This chapter shows the ship's officers at dinner. Meals are a rigid affair over which Ahab presides: no one talks, and a strict order of service is followed. After the officers finish eating, the table is relaid for the harpooners, who eat heartily, intimidating the cook with their voraciousness. The cabin is not a comfortable place for anyone, as it is Ahab's territory and Ahab is "inaccessible," "an alien."

CHAPTER 35: THE MAST-HEAD

Ishmael describes his first post on the masthead (the top of the ship's masts) watching for whales. He provides a history of mastheads and their role on whaling ships. He proceeds to discuss statues, hermits, and ancient Egyptians as prior "mast-head standers." The masthead is a place where whalers spend a great deal of time, and Ishmael laments its lack of comforts: on a South Seas ship, the masthead offers only two small pegs upon which to stand. He compares this setup to that of other ships, which have miniature cabins atop the masts. Ishmael admits that he himself daydreams too much to keep a good watch, and he warns captains against hiring "romantic, melancholy, and absent-minded young men," who are likely to miss whales in the vicinity.

CHAPTER 36: THE QUARTER-DECK (ENTER AHAB: THEN, ALL.)

Ahab finally makes an official appearance before the men. First, he stirs the crew by calling out simple questions about their mission, to which they respond in unison. He then presents a Spanish gold doubloon, proclaiming, "Whosoever of ye raises me a white-headed whale with a wrinkled brow and a crooked jaw . . . he shall have this gold ounce, my boys!" The men cheer, and the harpooners ask if it is Moby Dick that Ahab seeks. Ahab then confesses, in response to Starbuck's query, that it was indeed Moby Dick who stripped him of his leg, and he announces his quest to hunt the whale down. The men shout together that they will hunt with Ahab, though Starbuck protests that he "came here to hunt whales, not [his] commander's vengeance." Ahab commences a ritual that binds the crew together: he orders all of his men to drink from one flagon that gets passed around. Telling the harpooners to cross their lances before him, Ahab grasps the weapons and anoints Queequeg, Tashtego, and Daggoo "my three pagan kinsmen there—yon three most honorable gentlemen and noble men." He then makes them take the iron off of the harpoons to use as drinking goblets. They all drink together as Ahab proclaims, "God hunt us all, if we do not hunt Moby Dick to his death!"

CHAPTER 37: SUNSET

> *Over unsounded gorges, through the rifled hearts of*
> *mountains, under torrents' beds, unerringly I rush!*
> *(See* QUOTATIONS, *p. 75)*

"Sunset" begins with a stage direction that sets Ahab alone near a window and consists of a melancholy soliloquy by Ahab. He notes that everyone thinks that he is mad and that he agrees with them to a certain extent. He self-consciously calls himself "demoniac" and "madness maddened." He reveals that it was foretold that he would be dismembered by a whale. He proclaims, however, that he will be both "prophet" and "fulfiller" of Moby Dick's destiny. He accepts the inequality of the battle and challenges Moby Dick, claiming that the whale cannot avoid his fate: "The path to my fixed purpose is laid with iron rails, whereon my soul is grooved to run."

CHAPTER 38: DUSK

"Dusk" is Starbuck's monologue. Though he fears that all will turn out ill, he feels inextricably bound to Ahab, compelled to help him to "his impious end." When he hears the revelry coming from the crew's forecastle, he laments the whole doomed voyage and the "latent horror" in life.

CHAPTER 39: FIRST NIGHT-WATCH
"First Night-Watch" is Stubb's monologue, providing yet another perspective on the voyage. Stubb, believing all to be "predestinated," can only laugh and sing a ditty.

CHAPTER 40: MIDNIGHT, FORECASTLE
"Midnight, Forecastle" is scripted like a scene from a play and presents the sailors, all of different nationalities, showing off and singing together. They get into a fight when a Spanish sailor makes fun of Daggoo. The onset of a storm, however, halts their fighting and makes them tend to the ship. Pip asks the "big white God," who may be either God or Ahab, to "have mercy on this small black boy."

ANALYSIS: CHAPTERS 32–40
"Cetology" seems to be a grandiose digression, a way for Ishmael to show off his knowledge and his literary bent. The use of publishing terminology (the category names Folio, Octavo, and Duodecimo come from the different sizes of books produced by nineteenth-century printers) suggests the arbitrariness of human attempts to understand and classify the natural world. For Ishmael, though, the meaning lies not in the final classification but in the act of classifying, which signifies hope and resistance to futility. The classification also suggests that humans, in their imperfection, need such aids to understanding, lest they be lost in a deep and fathomless sea of information and phenomena.

With the statement of his quest, Ahab reveals his motivation to be considerably more complicated than resentment at losing his leg. Ahab's desire to strike at the world's malevolent agency indicates his profound intelligence and the philosophical reach of his mind; he looks for hidden realities beneath superficial appearances. At the same time, his sentiments suggest delusion and madness. One of the puzzling questions presented by his soliloquy is whether God is the malevolent agency against which Ahab seeks to strike out. Ahab echoes both Hamlet, in his probing of the metaphysical truths underlying everyday appearances, and Iago, in his absolute rejection of piety and morality and his manipulation of others in pursuit of his goal. In any case, Ahab strives to exceed the limits proscribed for human beings by conventional morality and religion.

Beginning with Chapter 36, the chapters in this section feature stage directions and other devices borrowed from plays. These elements heighten the reader's awareness that the book is becoming more dramatic: conflicts emerge between the characters, and Ahab self-consciously gives a performance to unite and manipulate his crew. These chapters often echo Shakespeare, both in their general style and in specific allusions to Shakespeare's plays. Ahab's soliloquy, in particular, masterfully imitates Shakespearean cadences and rhythms. Both Ahab and Starbuck are given soliloquy-style monologues in these chapters, each getting the chance to plead his case to the audience, as it were, as eloquently as he can.

CHAPTERS 41–47

CHAPTER 41: MOBY DICK

> *[A]ll evil, to crazy Ahab, were visibly personified, and made practically assailable in Moby Dick.*
> (See QUOTATIONS, *p. 76*)

Ishmael compares the legend of Moby Dick to his experience of the whale. He notes that sperm whale attacks have increased recently and that superstitious sailors have come to regard these attacks as having an intelligent, even supernatural origin. In particular, wild rumors about Moby Dick circulate among whalemen, suggesting that he can be in more than one place at the same time and that he is immortal. Ishmael remarks that even the wildest of rumors usually contains some truth. Whales, for instance, have been known to travel with remarkable speed from the Atlantic to the Pacific; thus, it is possible for a whale to be caught in the Pacific with the harpoons of a Greenland ship in it. Moby Dick, who has defied capture numerous times, exhibits an "intelligent malignity" in his attacks on men.

Ishmael explains that Ahab lost his leg when he tried to attack Moby Dick with a knife after the whale destroyed his boats. Far from land, Ahab did not have access to much in the way of medical care and thus underwent unimaginable physical and mental suffering on the ship's return to Nantucket. Ishmael deduces that Ahab's madness and his single-minded drive to destroy the whale must have originated during his bedridden agony.

CHAPTER 42: THE WHITENESS OF THE WHALE

Ishmael explains what Moby Dick meant to him at the time of the voyage: above all, it was the whiteness of the whale that appalled him. Ishmael begins his discussion of "whiteness" by noting its use as a symbol of virtue, nobility, and racial superiority. To him, the color white only multiplies the terror when it is attached to any object already "terrible" in and of itself, such as a shark or polar bear.

CHAPTER 43: HARK!
This chapter offers a short, dramatic dialogue between two sailors on watch. One thinks that he has heard a humanlike noise from the hold (where a ship's cargo is normally stowed). The other hears nothing, and the first reminds him that Stubb and others have whispered about a mysterious passenger in the hold.

CHAPTER 44: THE CHART
Ishmael describes Ahab's attempts to locate Moby Dick. Ahab believes that he can predict where the whale will be by tracing currents that the whale might follow in search of food. He is also aware that Moby Dick has been known to show up in a certain place at the same time every year. Ahab's single-minded focus occasionally leads him to burst into fits of near-mad shrieking. Ishmael speculates that these fits are the result of the remainder of Ahab's soul trying to escape from his demented psyche.

CHAPTER 45: THE AFFIDAVIT
Ishmael acknowledges that the reader may find the story thus far presented to be incredible and cites several items from his own experience and from written authorities to bolster the probability of his narrative. First, he demonstrates the uniqueness of individual whales and the frequency with which whales survive attack by humans. He then considers why people may not believe such stories: perhaps readers haven't heard about the perils or vivid adventures common to the whaling industry. He asks that the audience use "human reasoning" when judging his story and not read it as a "hideous and intolerable allegory."

CHAPTER 46: SURMISES
Ishmael considers the means by which Ahab will exact his revenge. Because Ahab must use men as his tools, he has to be careful to maintain their loyalty throughout the long sea voyage. Ahab knows that he can appeal to their emotions for a limited time but that cash is a more reliable motivator. He is acutely aware that his behavior leaves him open to the charge of "usurpation," since he has changed the purpose of the voyage from that which the ships' owners intended. He knows that he must aggressively pursue all sperm whales in his path or his officers will have grounds to relieve him of his command.

CHAPTER 47: THE MAT-MAKER

Ishmael describes the slow, dreamy atmosphere on the ship when it is not in pursuit of a whale. He and Queequeg make a sword-mat, and Ishmael likens their weaving to work on "the Loom of Time": the threads of the warp are fixed like necessity, and man has limited free will, as he can interweave his own cross-threads into this fixed structure. When Queequeg's sword hits the loom and alters the overall pattern, Ishmael calls this chance. He is jolted out of his reverie by Tashtego's sighting of a whale. Suddenly, everyone is busied in preparation for the whale hunt. Just as the men are about to push off in the harpoon boats, "five dusky phantoms" emerge around Ahab.

ANALYSIS: CHAPTERS 42–47

These chapters contain very little action, focusing instead on the meaning of the events already described. In the first place, Ishmael takes considerable pains to ensure that the reader will not interpret his story as a tall tale fabricated to impress the gullible. He demonstrates in great detail that a specific whale can be recognized, become the subject of rumor and legend, and even be hunted. His request that his narrative be taken literally and not as some "hideous and intolerable allegory" emphasizes that Ahab's desire to kill Moby Dick exists not on some symbolic level but rather in the realm of corporeal experience.

Ishmael's protestation against allegorical interpretation is obviously ironic, since the reader knows that Ishmael's story is fiction and has witnessed Ishmael's inordinate tendency to introduce an allegorical or metaphorical aspect into almost everything that his narrative touches. But Ishmael is also in earnest, as his exhaustive presentation of facts about whales demonstrates. The point of this irony seems to be that the events of the novel were not invented by an author (whether Melville or Ishmael) in order to communicate a single allegorical meaning. Rather, the novel presents events that could, apparently, happen and explores the different ways in which people—Ahab, Ishmael, the other sailors—interpret these same events. The movements of whales, like all of the secrets of the ocean, are largely hidden, and the whalemen's struggles to piece together what they see and hear resemble other people's struggles to make meaning out of life or stories in books.

Ishmael returns repeatedly to a scientific model to interpret various phenomena. He assembles a mass of empirical observations about whales and whaling and systematizes it, modifying the work of previous naturalists and leaving behind an account that could be modified by scientists after him. Moreover, he demonstrates that records of whale sightings form the subject of a captain's practical knowledge, so that whales can be actively and methodically hunted.

The symbolic or subjective meaning of Moby Dick's existence is a more complicated matter. The rumors circulated by the whalemen about Moby Dick's ubiquity and immortality seem rooted in a credulousness born of fear and superstition. Ahab's obsession with the whale is far more profound than that of the other sailors. He projects all of his intuitions about the presence of evil in the world onto the White Whale. Though Ishmael notes the inherent absurdity of this projection, his remark that other cultures have presumed the existence of malignant forces in the world suggests that Ahab's belief in an intelligent and malignant presence lurking behind creation is not necessarily wrong.

CHAPTERS 48–54

CHAPTER 48: THE FIRST LOWERING

As the crew launches the harpoon boats for the first time this voyage, Ahab's secret crew emerges from the hold and boards the captain's harpoon boat. Fedallah, their leader, is a dark, sinister figure with a Chinese jacket and a turban made from coiling his own hair around his head. With him are several more "tiger-yellow . . . natives of the Manillas" (the Philippines) who have been hiding in the hold of the *Pequod*. Ishmael recalls the shadowy figures that he saw boarding the ship in Nantucket, the strange noises that have been heard coming from the hold, and Ahab's frequent visits down there: all these phenomena are explained by the presence of Fedallah and his men. The harpoon boat crews stare at their newly discovered shipmates, but Flask tells them to continue doing their jobs—to concentrate on hunting the whale. The *Pequod*'s first lowering after a pod of whales is unsuccessful. Flask must stand on his harpooner Daggoo's shoulders because he is too short to see otherwise. Queequeg manages to land a harpoon in a whale, but the animal overturns the boat. The men in Queequeg's boat are nearly crushed by the ship as it passes looking for them, since a squall has cast mist over everything. Finally, however, they are pulled aboard.

CHAPTER 49: THE HYENA

Ishmael laughs at the absurdity of the situation in which he finds himself: he has never been on a whaling voyage before, and he is surprised at the danger that attends even an ordinary whale hunt. The *Pequod*'s mates tell him that they have hunted whales in much more dangerous conditions than those that Ishmael has just witnessed. Ishmael decides to rewrite his will and asks Queequeg to help him do so. He feels better afterward, and comes to a morbid understanding of himself as a man already dead: any additional time that he survives at sea will be a bonus.

CHAPTER 50: AHAB'S BOAT AND CREW · FEDALLAH

Ahab's decision to have his own harpoon boat and crew, says Ishmael, is not a typical practice in the whaling industry. Captains do not frequently risk themselves in pursuit of whales, and Ahab's injury makes it even more surprising that he would personally command a harpoon boat. Clearly the *Pequod*'s owners would not approve, which accounts for Ahab's secrecy about Fedallah and his plans. However strange, "in a whaler, wonders soon wane" because there are so many unconventional sights on such a voyage. Even though whalemen are not easily awestruck, they find Ahab's crew bizarre, and "[t]hat hair-turbaned Fedallah remained a muffled mystery to the last." Ishmael hints that there is something demoniacal about the man.

CHAPTER 51: THE SPIRIT-SPOUT

Looking down from the masthead one night, Fedallah thinks that he sees a whale spouting. The ship then tries to follow it but the whale is not seen again. Mysteriously, a similar spout is seen regularly each night from then on. Ishmael calls it a "spirit-spout" because it seems to be a phantom leading them on. Some think it might be Moby Dick leading the ship on toward its destruction. The *Pequod* sails around the Cape of Good Hope at the southern tip of Africa, a particularly treacherous passage. Through it all, Ahab commands the deck robustly and, even when he is down in the cabin, keeps his eye on the cabin compass that tells him where the ship is going. Between the phantom spout and the dangerous passage, the men resign themselves to being "practical fatalists."

CHAPTER 52: THE ALBATROSS

The men soon see a ship called the *Goney,* or *Albatross,* a vessel with a "spectral appearance" that has been at sea for four years. Ahab asks this ship's crew, as the two ships pass by, if they have seen Moby Dick. The other captain tries to respond, but a gust of wind blows the speaking trumpet from his mouth. The two ships' wakes cross as they continue on, and the schools of fish that have been following the *Pequod* turn to follow the *Albatross,* which saddens Ahab. The *Pequod* continues its way "around the world," and Ishmael ruminates that this grand-sounding mission really amounts to going in circles.

CHAPTER 53: THE GAM

Ishmael then explains why the *Pequod* and the *Albatross* did not have a "gam." Ishmael defines a gam as "*[a] social meeting of two (or more) Whale-ships, generally on a cruising-ground; when, after exchanging hails, they exchange visits by boats' crews: the two captains remaining, for the time, on board of one ship, and the two chief mates on the other.*" Ships typically exchange letters, reading material, and news of their relative successes. Ahab, however, desires gams only with ships whose captains have information about Moby Dick.

CHAPTER 54: THE TOWN-HO'S STORY (AS TOLD AT THE GOLDEN INN.)

Ishmael narrates a story about another ship, the *Town-Ho,* that was originally told to Tashtego during a gam between the *Town-Ho* and the *Pequod.* Ishmael announces at the beginning of the chapter that he gives the reader the version that he once told to some Spanish friends in Lima. The basic story concerns Radney, a mate from Martha's Vineyard, and Steelkilt, a sailor from Buffalo, who have a conflict on board the *Town-Ho,* a sperm whaler from Nantucket. Steelkilt rebels against Radney's authority, assaults him after being provoked, and starts a mutiny. The mutineers are captured, flogged, and released, but Steelkilt wants revenge against Radney, who flogged him when the captain would not. The *Town-Ho* encounters Moby Dick before Steelkilt can murder Radney, though, and, in the process of trying to harpoon the whale, Radney falls out of the boat. Moby Dick snatches him in his jaws. Ishmael's Peruvian listeners have a hard time believing the story, but he swears on a Bible that he is telling the truth and claims to have met and spoken with Steelkilt.

ANALYSIS: CHAPTERS 48–54

The appearance of Fedallah and his men changes the dynamic aboard the *Pequod.* Fedallah is an anomaly even in the culturally diverse whaling industry, and Ishmael describes him as a "muffled mystery to the last." Early in the novel, when Ishmael witnesses Fedallah and the others slipping aboard the ship, and Elijah ominously alludes to them, it seems as if the *Pequod* has been boarded by ghosts or devils. Now Ishmael realizes that they are quite real, although they remain mysterious because of their aloofness and their connection to Ahab. Throughout the narrative, the reader finds it difficult to extricate the real from the supernatural, in part because Ahab exploits mystery and superstition for his own ends.

The concept of fate, in particular, serves Ahab's purposes, as he manipulates the crew into accepting that the hunt for the White Whale is their destiny. Fatalism, the belief in the inevitability of fate, is a perverse comfort to the sailors, enabling them to set aside their fears during times of danger since they believe that what will happen to them has already been determined by an external force. However, this supposed comfort doesn't stop the crew from looking for signs of their fate. The phantom spout, the fish that turn away from the *Pequod* to follow the *Albatross,* and the death of Radney in "The *Town-Ho's* Story" all foreshadow a catastrophic end to the *Pequod*'s quest. For Ishmael, acknowledging these signs and coming to terms with the extraordinary dangers of whaling brings a sense of relief. His belief in a predetermined fate lets him appreciate the present, and he comes to consider each new day as a gift.

Ahab, unlike his crew, views fate not as an externally determined destiny but as a way to justify his own perverse actions. He uses the idea of fate to motivate his crew and actively tries to determine his own "fate." Moby Dick will not find Ahab; rather, Ahab must seek Moby Dick out. For Ahab, fate is a fiction that allows him to pursue his vengeance: most of what he calls fate is the result of deliberately planned action.

The two "gams" in this section of the book are the first in a series of inset stories that come out of encounters with other ships. The gams highlight Ahab's unhealthy obsession by reminding the reader that men other than Ahab have encountered Moby Dick without reacting so irrationally to the experience. Gams are part of the normal social order of the seafaring world, and Ahab's unwillingness to participate in them unless he can use them to glean information relevant to his quest accentuates his eccentricity. The narrative uses gams to build a more complete picture of the maritime community: stories are traded, legends grow, and the social codes of the sailors are put on display.

Chapters 55–65

Chapter 55: Of the Monstrous Pictures of Whales
Ishmael considers well-known graphic depictions of whales. To a whaleman who has actually seen whales, most historical, mythological, and scientific sources are blatantly inaccurate. As a result, says Ishmael, "you must needs conclude that the great Leviathan is that one creature in the world which must remain unpainted to the last." The only solution that Ishmael sees for one who seeks to know what a whale looks like is an actual encounter with the creature. In the ocean, only portions of a whale are visible at any one time, the majority of the animal being underwater. Only dead whales are visible in their near-entirety, and those are to the living animal what a wrecked ship is to one afloat. He warns the reader not to "be too fastidious in your curiosity" about the whale, since such curiosity is unlikely to be satisfied.

Chapter 56: Of the Less Erroneous Pictures of Whales, and the True Pictures of Whaling Scenes
Ishmael then tries to find some acceptable depictions of whales. To his mind, the only pictures that come close are two large French engravings that show the sperm and right whales in action. He wonders why the French have been best able to capture whales and whaling in art, because France is not a whaling nation.

Chapter 57: Of Whales in Paint; In Teeth; In Wood; In Sheet-Iron; In Stone; In Mountains; In Stars
Ishmael considers versions of whales crafted by whalers, including specimens carved in ivory, wood, and metal. Those with an interest in the creature can see whales everywhere, including in geological forms and in the starry sky.

Chapter 58: Brit
Brit is a minute yellow substance upon which the right whale feeds. Ishmael moves from a discussion of feeding whales to a generalized comparison between the land and the sea. In the sea, there are hidden horrors and continuous danger, while on land, all is visible and therefore manageable. He applies this assessment to the human soul, which he believes contains a small island of "peace and joy" surrounded by an ocean of horrors.

CHAPTER 59: SQUID

As the *Pequod* sails toward Java, Daggoo thinks that he sights Moby Dick. The boats are lowered and the animal pursued. It is a false alarm, however, as it is only a giant squid, which is taken as a bad omen. Ishmael notes that the squid is conjectured to be the sperm whale's food, but that the sperm whale feeds and lives largely out of sight beneath the sea's surface.

CHAPTER 60: THE LINE

In preparation for a later scene, says Ishmael, he will describe the whale-line. Made of hemp, this rope is connected to the harpoon at one end and dangles free at the other so that it can be tied to other boats' lines. Because it is laid out throughout the boat and whizzes out when a whale is darted, it is dangerous for the men of the harpoon crews. All men, according to Ishmael, live with metaphorical whale-lines around their necks, and it is only when a catastrophe occurs that they realize the constant perils of life.

CHAPTER 61: STUBB KILLS A WHALE

Queequeg views the squid as a good omen, indicating the presence of a sperm whale nearby. The crew soon sights a spouting sperm whale, which Stubb and Tashtego succeed in killing.

CHAPTER 62: THE DART

Ishmael gives a quick account of the harpooning of a whale. He argues that the system presently in use is inefficient, as the harpooner is forced to row strenuously before harpooning the whale and is thus breathing too hard to aim properly.

CHAPTER 63: THE CROTCH

The crotch is a wooden support for a harpoon. Ishmael quickly digresses from describing the crotch to consider the loose harpoons that pose a threat to the boats. Each line has two harpoons attached to it. Ideally, both would be thrown and stuck into the whale. More commonly, however, the whale dives after the first strike and the second harpoon must be thrown overboard to prevent injury to those in the boat. Dangling loose in the water, the second harpoon still poses a great danger to the boats.

CHAPTER 64: STUBB'S SUPPER

Most whalemen do not enjoy whale meat; Stubb, however, wants to dine on a steak from his whale. While he devours his steak, sharks dine on the carcass of the whale, which has been tied fast to the ship.

Stubb calls on the black cook, Fleece, to make his supper; he also demands that the cook order the sharks to stop eating the whale flesh. The cook delivers a sermon to the sharks, telling them that they ought to be more civilized. Stubb then proceeds to torment the cook, who likens Stubb to a shark.

CHAPTER 65: THE WHALE AS A DISH

Ishmael offers a culinary history of the whale. He remarks that no one except for Stubb and the Eskimos still eat it. Deterrents include the exceedingly rich quality of the meat and its prodigious quantities. Furthermore, it seems wrong to eat whale because, though hunting the whale makes the meat a "noble dish," one has to eat the meat by the light of a lamp that burns the whale's oil. But, Ishmael ponders, perhaps this adding of insult to injury isn't so rare: his readers probably eat beef with a knife made from the bone of oxen and pick their teeth after eating goose with a goose feather.

ANALYSIS: CHAPTERS 55–65

The chapters that survey visual depictions of whales demonstrate the cultural ubiquity of whales while simultaneously questioning the accuracy of pictures, and perhaps all representations, in general. Ishmael questions whether it is possible to create an object that conveys the reality and the spirit of the whale and its hunters. In doing so, he may implicitly suggest that his own picture of the whale—his narrative—will be inadequate. Alternatively, he may mean to imply the superiority of a picture in words to a graphic representation. The few engravings and paintings that Ishmael praises seem to be effective because they offer dramatic but not necessarily realistic scenes and convey some of the terror involved in a close encounter with a whale, which can also be said of Ishmael's narrative.

The sea, which offers only its surface for interpretation while hiding unknown events in its depths, is a perfect model of human perception. As Ishmael notes in Chapter 58 with his metaphor for the human soul, even when we examine ourselves, we see only surfaces and quick glimpses of hidden truths. Ishmael finds this limitation to human perception strangely liberating. Unaware of what lies beneath these surfaces, he is free to interpret the world as he sees fit. His narration in these chapters tends to begin with a discussion of something concrete like brit or the giant squid before veering into philosophical speculation about concepts like the human soul and the mysteries of the ocean.

Ishmael also offers the first of many digressions about whaling equipment and technique in these chapters. After describing the successful hunt of a whale, Ishmael goes back to talk about the crotch where a whale dart rests. His explanations about equipment and history give the novel a realistic and precise feel. This use of detail acts as a bulwark against the perceptual and philosophical uncertainty that threatens Ishmael's narrative. As a result, the novel at times reads more like a documentary than a work of fiction.

These chapters also include comic relief, in the person of the cook Fleece (whose name likely reflects the nineteenth-century American description of black people's hair as "woolly"). The cook's sermon to the sharks contrasts with Father Mapple's sermon in Chapter 9. Whereas Mapple delivers a lofty theological sermon full of metaphor and high ideals, Fleece addresses the sharks as "fellow-critters" and makes a series of startling points about equality, social justice, and the importance of distributing resources equally. Though it is supposed to be funny, his sermon resonates with Ishmael's mention of sharks following slave ships for a taste of their human cargo and with Stubb's mistreatment of the black Fleece. Fleece instances the undercurrent of racism and abuse within the supposedly meritocratic order aboard the *Pequod*.

CHAPTERS 66–73

CHAPTER 66: THE SHARK MASSACRE
The crew lashes the sperm whale they have caught to the side of the ship to be dealt with in daylight. But the men are forced to poke with spades or kill the numerous sharks that attempt to devour the whale carcass. Ishmael warns that it is unwise "to meddle with the corpses and ghosts of these creatures": Queequeg nearly has his hand cut off by the sharp teeth of one dead shark hoisted onto the ship for its skin.

CHAPTER 67: CUTTING IN
The gory business of "cutting-in," or processing the whale, commences. The cutting-in involves inserting a hook in the whale's blubber and peeling the blubber off as one might peel off an orange rind in one strip.

CHAPTER 68: THE BLANKET
As he describes the whale's blubber, Ishmael argues that this strip of flesh is actually the whale's skin. A thin and cellophane-like layer

may be observed outside of the blubber, but this layer is only the skin of the skin. Ishmael admires the whale for its "thick walls," which allow it to live without being affected by its environment.

CHAPTER 69: THE FUNERAL

After the cutting-in, the whale is released for its "funeral," in which the "mourners" are vultures and sharks. The frightful white carcass floats away, and a "vengeful ghost" hovers over it, deterring other ships from going near it. Frequently, floating whale corpses are mistaken for rocks and shoals and thus entered on mariners' charts, causing future whalers to avoid the area. The whale thus continues to inspire terror even in death.

CHAPTER 70: THE SPHYNX

Ishmael describes the "scientific anatomical feat" of the whale's beheading, which occurs before the carcass is released; the head holds the valuable spermaceti, from which the finest oil comes. While the crew takes a break for a meal, Ahab talks to the whale's head hanging at the ship's side, asking it to tell him of the horrors that it has seen.

CHAPTER 71: THE JEROBOAM'S STORY

While Ahab converses with the whale, the *Jeroboam,* another whaling ship, sails into sight. An epidemic has broken out aboard her, so her captain doesn't board the *Pequod* but brings a small boat alongside for a talk with Ahab. Stubb recognizes one of the men at the oars of the boat as a man about whom he has heard from the crew of the *Town-Ho* during the last gam. This man, who had been a prophet among the Shakers in New York, proclaimed himself the archangel Gabriel on the ship, ordered the captain to jump overboard, and mesmerized the crew. The *Jeroboam*'s skipper, Captain Mayhew, wanted to get rid of Gabriel at the next port, but the crew threatened to desert if he was put ashore.

The sailors aboard the *Pequod* now see this very Gabriel in front of them. As Captain Mayhew tells Ahab a story about the White Whale, Gabriel interrupts continually. According to Mayhew, he and his men first heard about the existence of Moby Dick when they were speaking to another ship. Gabriel then warned against killing it, calling it "the Shaker God incarnated." They ran into Moby Dick a year later, and the ship's leaders decided to hunt it. As a mate stood in the ship to throw his lance, the whale flipped the mate into the air and tossed him into the sea. No one was harmed except for the mate, who drowned.

Gabriel had watched this episode from the masthead. The apparent fulfillment of his prophecy has led the crew to become his disciples. When Ahab confirms that he still intends to hunt the White Whale, Gabriel points to him, saying, "Think, think of the blasphemer—dead, and down there!—beware of the blasphemer's end!" Ahab realizes that the *Pequod* is carrying a letter for the dead mate and tries to hand it over to Captain Mayhew on the end of a cutting-spade pole. Gabriel manages to grab it, impales it on the boat-knife, and sends it back to Ahab's feet as the *Jeroboam*'s boat pulls away.

CHAPTER 72: THE MONKEY-ROPE

Ishmael backtracks to explain how Queequeg initially inserts the blubber hook into the whale for the cutting-in. Ishmael, as Queequeg's bowsman, ties the monkey-rope around his own waist, "wedding" himself to Queequeg, who is on the whale's floating body trying to attach the hook. (In a footnote, we learn that only on the *Pequod* were the monkey and this holder actually tied together, an improvement introduced by Stubb, who found that it increases the reliability of the holder.) While Ishmael holds Queequeg, Tashtego and Daggoo brandish their whale-spades to keep the sharks away. When Dough-Boy, the steward, offers Queequeg some tepid ginger and water, the mates frown at the influence of pesky Temperance activists and make the steward bring him alcohol. The remainder of the ginger, a gift from "Aunt Charity," a Nantucket matron, is thrown overboard.

CHAPTER 73: STUBB AND FLASK KILL A RIGHT WHALE; AND THEN HAVE A TALK OVER HIM

The *Pequod* spots a right whale. After killing the whale, Stubb asks Flask what Ahab might want with this "lump of foul lard" (right whales were far less valuable than sperm whales). Flask responds that Fedallah says that a whaler with a sperm whale's head on her starboard side and a right whale's head on her larboard will never capsize afterward. They then both confess that they don't like Fedallah and think of him as "the devil in disguise." The right whale's head is lifted onto the opposite side of the boat from the sperm whale's head, and, in fact, the *Pequod* settles into balance. As Ishmael observes, however, the ship would float even better with neither head there. He observes Fedallah standing in Ahab's shadow and notes that Fedallah's shadow "seem[s] to blend with, and lengthen Ahab's."

ANALYSIS: CHAPTERS 66–73

This series of chapters juxtaposes the practical matters of whaling with a series of perceptual problems. The sharks that swarm around the boat seem to possess malevolent agency even after they are killed. Whale carcasses find their way into ships' logs as rocks or shoals, giving rise to long-lasting errors. Ishmael argues that the whale's blubber is its skin, but his argument suggests that any such classification of the whale's parts must be arbitrary. Such difficulties suggest that mistakes and misreadings cannot be avoided, and that comparison and approximation are the only means by which things can be described.

Instead of anthropomorphizing the whale—that is, assigning it human characteristics—Ishmael takes features of the whale and presents them as potential models for human life. He admires and envies the whale's blubber, which insulates the whale and enables it to withstand its environment, as evidenced by his cry of "Oh, man! admire and model thyself after the whale!" For Ishmael, however, the human acquiring of such an attribute has metaphorical significance: the idea of "remain[ing] warm among ice" hearkens back to the image, in Chapter 58, of the soul's small island of "peace and joy" amid terrorizing oceans. With its "rare virtue of a strong individual vitality," then, the whale, unlike man, according to Ishmael, exists in a sort of bliss of perfection, self-possession, and independence.

These chapters return to the topic of male bonding and homoeroticism explored in the early stages of the relationship between Queequeg and Ishmael. The monkey rope—"an elongated Siamese ligature"—connects the two men as if they were twins. They are joined in a "wedding" once again and, "should poor Queequeg sink to rise no more, then both usage and honor demand . . . that instead of cutting the cord, it should drag [Ishmael] down in his wake." This new bond makes the "till death do us part" clause of the Christian marriage ceremony literal: only death can sever the tie that binds Ishmael to Queequeg at this moment. As they depend on one another for their very lives, the bonds between the two are stronger than the relationship they had back on land. These men know they can trust one another because that trust is tested on a daily basis. This all-male world is more egalitarian, more open, and even more loving than the heterosexual world back home. By using the vocabulary of love and marriage—the primary relationships in our society—to describe the bonds between these men, Melville suggests that these shipboard pairings are models of ideal partnership.

The encounter with the *Jeroboam* is one of the most important of the series of visits that the *Pequod* entertains from other ships. The introduction of a group of outsiders provides perspective on the actions of Ahab and his crew. The appearance of the crazed prophet Gabriel invites the reader to compare Gabriel's mental state to that of Ahab and Fedallah: each of these characters claims to possess prophetic or occult knowledge, but each of them may be crazy.

CHAPTERS 74–81

CHAPTER 74: THE SPERM WHALE'S HEAD— CONTRASTED VIEW

The two whale heads hanging from the *Pequod* provide an opportunity for Ishmael to give a lesson on "practical cetology." The sperm whale has a great well of sperm, ivory teeth, a long lower jaw, and one external spout hole. Ishmael describes the sperm whale as having "more character" than the right whale, as well as a "pervading dignity" based on the "mathematical symmetry" of its head. He wonders at the whale's small eyes, which are placed on opposite sides of its head, affording the whale a strange visual perspective. He notes also that the external portion of the whale's ear is tiny, comprised of only a small pinhole.

CHAPTER 75: THE RIGHT WHALE'S HEAD— CONTRASTED VIEW

The right whale, on the other hand, Ishmael explains, has bones in its mouth shaped like Venetian blinds, a huge lower lip, a tongue, and two external spout holes. He likens the right whale to a Stoic and the sperm whale to a "Platonian."

CHAPTER 76: THE BATTERING-RAM

Ishmael then points out that the blunt, large, wall-like part of the sperm whale's head seems to be just a "wad." In actuality, inside the thin, sturdy casing is a "mass of tremendous life." Ishmael notes that the whale's head, like many other things in nature, derives its strength from its flexibility and ability to be compressed and change shape.

CHAPTER 77: THE GREAT HEIDELBURGH TUN

Ishmael continues his survey by noting that the upper part of a whale's head has two subdivisions: the case and the junk. He compares the case to the "Great Heidelburgh Tun," a famous German wine vessel of enormous capacity. The case—which contains a reservoir of highly prized spermaceti, a valuable waxlike substance found in the oil—is carefully tapped once the whale's head has been suspended out of the water. The junk also contains oil, but this oil is trapped in a honeycomb of tough fibers.

Chapter 78: Cistern and Buckets

Ishmael describes Tashtego's tapping of the case. The sperm that it contains is lifted from the whale's head, which still dangles alongside the ship, to the deck by a relay of buckets. In tapping this whale, Tashtego accidentally falls into the case, which is at least twenty feet deep. In a panic, Daggoo clears the tangled lines and tries to get a line inside the head to Tashtego, but the tackle holding the head aloft breaks, and the great mass falls into the ocean. Queequeg dives in and manages to save Tashtego by cutting into the slowly sinking head and "delivering" Tashtego as a doctor would a baby.

Chapter 79: The Prairie

Ishmael applies the nineteenth-century arts of physiognomy (the art of judging human character from facial features) and phrenology (the study of the shape of the skull, based on the belief that it reveals character and mental capacity) to the whale. He considers the whale's features and, by means of physiognomic and phrenological analysis, concludes that the sperm whale's large, clear brow gives it the dignity of a god and that its "pyramidical silence" demonstrates its genius. But Ishmael then abandons this line of analysis, saying that he isn't a professional, and dares the reader to decipher the "hieroglyphics" of the sperm whale's brow.

Chapter 80: The Nut

Ishmael then turns to the whale's skull, calling the whale's brow "false" because there really isn't much in the skull besides the sperm—its brain is only about ten inches across and is hidden behind some twenty feet of forehead. Ishmael then says that he would rather feel a man's spine than his skull to try to know him. If creatures were judged by their spines rather than their brains, he argues, people would discount the smallness of the whale's brain and admire the magnitude of his spinal cord. He believes that the whale's hump signifies its indomitable spirit.

Chapter 81: The Pequod Meets the Virgin

The *Jungfrau* (Virgin) is out of oil, as she has had no success in catching whales. Her captain boards the *Pequod* to beg for some. Ahab asks about the White Whale, but the *Jungfrau* has no information.

Almost immediately after the captain of the *Jungfrau* steps off the *Pequod*'s deck, whales are sighted, and the captain goes after them desperately. The *Pequod* also gives chase and succeeds in harpooning a slower whale before the Germans can catch it. The whale is old, blind, and covered with growths, and in its flesh the crew finds an ancient-looking stone harpoon point. After bringing the carcass alongside the ship, the crew discovers that the whale is sinking and dragging the ship down with it. Ishmael then notes that it is impossible to predict which whales will sink. The inexperienced crew of the *Jungfrau* then starts chasing a finback, a whale that to the unskilled observer resembles a sperm whale but is too fast a swimmer to be caught.

ANALYSIS: CHAPTERS 74–81

Though he attempts simply to describe the whale heads accurately, Ishmael is soon tempted into making imaginative comparisons between the heads and schools of classical philosophy (Stoic and "Platonian.") Additionally, phrenology and physiognomy, popular in the nineteenth century, are only pseudoscientific. Physiognomy was widely used in the study of criminal behavior and as a justification of discrimination against the poor and against certain racial groups. Likewise, phrenology was also used to justify racial inequality, and gave rise to the judgmental terms "highbrow" and "lowbrow." As such, these disciplines, which developed out of subjective and therefore biased principles, hardly constitute rational inquiry.

As he considers the whale, Ishmael continuously probes deeper. From the outer surface of the skin, he moves in to the blubber; from the outer skull, he moves in to the "nut" or brain. This inward progression suggests an attempt to get at the heart, or inner meaning, of things and recalls Ahab's statement that he must "strike through the mask," or outward appearance. Ishmael explicitly connects this mode of investigation to reading. Phrenology and physiognomy, he says, are simply alternate forms of reading; instead of reading books, one reads skulls and faces. In saying "I but put that brow before you. Read it if you can," Ishmael offers a challenge to his reader to make sense of the bumps and curves of *Moby-Dick*. The connection between reading and these pseudosciences is a warning, though, that reading is subject to the reader's own biases. The multiplicity of readings of the whale's head, each based on a different discipline or a different set of principles, is a reminder that any single approach is insufficient and that an interdisciplinary approach may yield the most fruitful interpretations.

The rescue of Tashtego from the sinking whale's head is one of the most unusual moments of the novel, both in terms of the action itself and the language used to describe it. Ishmael describes the process as a rebirth, an exercise in "obstetrics." This depiction recalls Ishmael's earlier notion that whalers are men already dead. Tashtego, like the biblical Lazarus, has died and been reborn, and any extra days of his life are a gift. His rebirth also parodies religious images of resurrection. Tashtego is "delivered" from death not by Christ but by a fellow man—a non-Christian at that. Finally, Ishmael's obstetrics comparison points to a heightened level of linguistic play that characterizes much of the rest of the novel. As the men of the *Pequod* work together, their experience comes to encompass metaphorically all aspects of life, from birth to sexual maturation to death. Ishmael's language reflects this broad experience and mediates between the crude speech of real sailors, the aesthetic demands of the novel, and the genteel sensibilities of Melville's nineteenth-century reader.

Juxtaposed as it is with Tashtego's rescue, the encounter with the *Jungfrau* is subtly humorous, as the "virgin" ship would have no need for an obstetrician. The *Jungfrau* and the *Pequod* can be read, respectively, as innocence and experience. The naive *Jungfrau* chases illusions and engages in frivolous activities, while the more worldly *Pequod* austerely chases death. The whale for which the *Pequod* competes against the *Jungfrau* provides one of the most dramatic incidents of foreshadowing in the narrative so far. As if out of vengeance for its death, the whale seems to intentionally sink the *Pequod*. Given the description of the dying whale that Ishmael has just offered, in which he details the creature's humanlike suffering, this seeming vengeance is not at all surprising—the natural world is as vengeful as Ahab.

CHAPTERS 82–92

CHAPTER 82: THE HONOR AND GLORY OF WHALING
Ishmael considers the heroic history of whaling. He draws from Greek mythology, popular British legend, the Judeo-Christian Bible, and Hindu mythology: Perseus, St. George, Hercules, Jonah, and Vishnu (whose name Melville spells "Vishnoo") can all be considered whalemen based on the stories told about their exploits.

CHAPTER 83: JONAH HISTORICALLY REGARDED
Ishmael examines the Jonah story—which has shadowed the novel ever since the "Extracts" and Father Mapple's sermon in New Bedford—through the eyes of an old Sag Harbor whaleman who questions the tale based on his personal experience. Sag Harbor, as Ishmael calls him, doesn't believe that a whale of the kind described in the Bible could swallow a man, and he thinks that a whale's gastric juices would not permit a man to survive in the whale's stomach. Ishmael details various theologians' arcane responses to such practical questions.

CHAPTER 84: PITCHPOLING
Ishmael describes the process of oiling a harpoon boat's underside to increase speed. He reports that Queequeg performs this task carefully, seemingly with an awareness that the *Pequod* will encounter whales later that day. Stubb harpoons a fast and tireless whale. In order to capture it, he must "pitchpole" it by throwing a long lance from the jerking boat to secure the running whale. Stubb's lance strikes home, and the whale spouts blood.

CHAPTER 85: THE FOUNTAIN
With an attempt at scientific precision, Ishmael discusses how whales spout. He cannot define exactly what the spout is, so he has to put forward a hypothesis: the spout is nothing but mist, like the "semi-visible steam" emitted from the head of such ponderous beings as Plato, Pyrrho, the Devil, Jupiter, Dante, and even himself.

CHAPTER 86: THE TAIL
Ishmael then considers the opposite end of the animal, celebrating the whale's most famous part: its tail. He admires its combination of power and grace, and muses that it represents the whale's attempts to reach to heaven—the tail is often seen protruding toward the skies. Whether this positioning is viewed as an act of angelic adoration or demoniac defiance (like the shaking of a fist) on the whale's part depends on the mood of the spectator. Ishmael notes that the tail is the sperm whale's most frequent means of inflicting injury upon men.

CHAPTER 87: THE GRAND ARMADA
When the *Pequod* sails through the straits of Sunda (near Indonesia) without pulling into any port, Ishmael takes the opportunity to discuss the isolation and self-containment of a whaling ship. While in the straits, the *Pequod* encounters a great herd of sperm whales

swimming in a circle (the "Grand Armada"), but, as the ship chases the whales, it is itself pursued by Malay pirates. The *Pequod* escapes the pirates and launches boats after the whales, somehow ending up inside their circle, a placid lake. One harpooned whale flounders in pain, causing panic among the whole herd. The boats in the middle are in danger but manage to escape the chaos. They "drugg" the whales by attaching lines with large blocks of wood attached, which provide resistance and tire the swimming whales. The whalemen also try to "waif" the whales, marking them with pennoned poles as the *Pequod*'s, to be taken later. They succeed in capturing only one whale.

CHAPTER 88: SCHOOLS AND SCHOOLMASTERS

Ishmael takes a moment to explain some whaling terms, beginning with "schools" of whales. Schools are typically composed of one male—the "schoolmaster" or "lord"—and numerous females, the "harem." When whalers find a school, they hunt only the females and calves, as the males are too large and dangerous. As the male whales age, they leave their harems behind and become solitary, ill-tempered wanderers. The all-male schools are like a "mob of young collegians." The major difference between the males and the females, according to Ishmael, is that males abandon injured comrades while females do not, even risking their own lives to aid and comfort a friend.

CHAPTER 89: FAST-FISH AND LOOSE-FISH

Ishmael takes some time to explain his reference to "waifs" in Chapter 87. He goes on to talk about whaling codes past and present, which say that a "Fast-Fish" belongs to the party fast to it (the party that has laid claim to it) and a "Loose-Fish" is fair game for anybody who can catch it. A fish is "fast" when it is physically connected to the party after it or when it bears a waif, or marker. Lawyerlike, Ishmael cites precedents and stories to show how difficult it is to maintain rules, especially when they admit so much ambiguity. Metaphorically, everything in the world can be conceptualized according to the code that judges possession to be the sole legal criterion of ownership. Even entire nations, Ishmael observes, can be classified as "Fast-Fish" or "Loose-Fish" and colonized accordingly by more powerful nations.

CHAPTER 90: HEADS OR TAILS

Ishmael elaborates upon the strange fishing laws of England, which state that any whale or sturgeon captured on its coast is "fast" and belongs to England. The head must be given to the king and the tail to the queen, leaving nothing for the hunter. Ishmael tells the story of some poor whalemen who lost all profits from their hard-earned whale to a wealthy duke.

CHAPTER 91: THE PEQUOD MEETS THE ROSE-BUD

The *Pequod* encounters a French ship, the *Bouton de Rose* (Rose-Button or Rose-Bud), from which a terrible stench arises. This ship has two whales alongside: one "blasted whale" (a whale that died unmolested on the sea) that is going to have nothing useful in it and one whale that died from indigestion. Stubb asks a sailor aboard the *Rose-Bud* if they have any news of Moby Dick. The man answers that they have never heard of the White Whale. Crafty Stubb asks why the man is trying to get oil out of these whales when clearly there is none in either. The sailor replies that his captain, on his first trip, will not believe the sailor's own statements that the whales are worthless. Stubb goes aboard to tell the captain that the whales are worthless, although he knows something that the other sailor doesn't: the second whale might contain ambergris, a valuable substance found in the intestines of sick whales. Stubb gets the sailor to help him trick the French captain into thinking that the "blasted" whales pose a threat of infection to the crew. The captain dumps the whales and Stubb, pretending to be helpful, has the *Pequod*'s boats tow the second whale away. As soon as the *Rose-Bud* leaves, Stubb ties up to the second whale and finds the sweet-smelling ambergris inside it.

CHAPTER 92: AMBERGRIS

Ishmael explains that ambergris, though it looks like mottled cheese and comes from the bowels of whales, is actually used for perfumes. He ponders the origin of the idea that whales smell bad. In the past, whaling vessels were unable to render blubber into oil at sea, and the rotting blubber created a powerful stench when they arrived in port. The rendered oil, however, is odorless and a natural cleanser. Ishmael notes that live whales, like beautiful women, actually smell pleasantly musky.

ANALYSIS: CHAPTERS 82–92

Chapters 82 and 83 explore ways in which texts are misread and distorted. The story of Jonah is the subject of Father Mapple's sermon in Chapter 9, and Mapple himself might be regarded as the ideal reader. His imagination seizes upon what is important in a story without getting bogged down in extraneous details. Sag Harbor, in contrast, is so lost in technical objections that he misses the symbolic meaning of the Jonah story. The theologians whom Ishmael cites to counter Sag Harbor seem equally ludicrous, since they too ignore the story's underlying message, spinning ever more contorted explanations to maintain that every detail of the story is true. In Chapter 82, Ishmael himself is guilty of similar distortions when he ignores the totality of the careers of Hercules, St. George, and others to argue that they are whalemen.

The imagery in this section stresses ambiguity. Death and birth are connected as the blood of the panicked, hurt whales mingles with the milk that the calves are drinking when the "Grand Armada" of whales is attacked. When the *Pequod* chases the whales, it is in turn chased by pirates, illustrating that ocean life involves a repeating cycle of events; we thus come to understand the story of the *Pequod* from a larger, more philosophical perspective. This interchangeability of parts also suggests some equivalence between the men on the *Pequod* and the whales. Indeed, particularly in the chapter on "Schools and Schoolmasters," Ishmael gives the whale a range of human qualities. This anthropomorphizing (giving human attributes to nonhuman entities) suggests that hunting whales is exploitative and even murderous. Critics have suggested that *Moby-Dick* can be read as an analogue to other forms of exploitation by white men, such as slavery, colonialism, and territorial expansion.

CHAPTERS 93–101

CHAPTER 93: THE CASTAWAY

Pip, the *Pequod*'s cabin boy, is drafted to be a replacement oarsman in Stubb's harpoon boat. Having performed passably the first time out, Pip goes out in the harpoon boat a second time. This time, however, he jumps from the boat in fear when the whale raps the bottom of the boat beneath his seat. Pip's boatmates become angry when they have to cut the whale loose in order to save Pip after he gets tangled in the lines. Stubb tells him never to jump out of the boat again, threatening not to pick him up next time. But Pip does jump again, and to teach him a lesson, Stubb leaves him alone in the middle of the sea's "heartless immensity." This experience drives him mad, at least insofar as his shipmates can observe. Ishmael, on the other hand, declares that the experience endows Pip with divine wisdom.

CHAPTER 94: A SQUEEZE OF THE HAND

Because the spermaceti taken from a whale's head quickly cools into lumps, the sailors have to squeeze it back into liquid. Ishmael is carried away with enthusiasm for the "sweet and unctuous" sperm. He squeezes all morning long, sentimentally describing his physical contact with the other sailors, whose hands he unintentionally gropes in the vat of sperm. He also describes some of the other tissues of the whale from which oil is derived. He gives a brief glimpse into the ship's "blubber-room," where the blubber is cut into sections and prepared for rendering. The blubber-room is a dark and dangerous place: the blubber-men frequently lose toes to the sharp spades used to cut the blubber.

CHAPTER 95: THE CASSOCK

Ishmael describes the other parts of the whale, including the penis, euphemistically named the "cassock." He blasphemously likens the whale's organ to the dress of clergymen because it has some pagan mysticism attached to it. It also serves a practical purpose on the ship: the mincer wears the black "pelt" of skin from the penis to protect himself while he slices the pieces of blubber for the pots.

CHAPTER 96: THE TRY-WORKS

> [E]ven in his lowest swoop the mountain eagle is still
> higher than other birds upon the plain, even though
> they soar.
>
> (See QUOTATIONS, p. 77)

Ishmael attempts to explain the try-works, a set of pots and furnaces that boil the blubber and derive all the oil from it. He associates the try-works with darkness and a sense of exotic evil: it has "an unspeakable, wild, Hindoo odor about it, such as may lurk in the vicinity of funereal pyres." Furthermore, the pagan harpooners tend it. Ishmael comments that the hellish red fires of the try-works, combined with the black sea and the dark night, so disorient him that he loses his sense of himself at the tiller. Everything becomes "inverted," he says, and suddenly there is "no compass before me to steer by."

CHAPTER 97: THE LAMP

Whalemen are always in the light, Ishmael explains, because their job is to collect oil from the seas. These men have free access to the oil, and each keeps a collection of lamps in his bunk. The interior of the ship is illuminated like a temple.

CHAPTER 98: STOWING DOWN AND CLEARING UP

Ishmael completes his description of how whale oil is processed. The oil is put in casks and the ship is cleaned. Here he dismisses another myth about whaling, asserting that whalers are *not* inherently dirty. Sperm whale oil, in fact, is a fine cleaning agent. Ishmael must admit, however, that whalers are clean for barely a day when the next whale is sighted and the cycle begins again.

CHAPTER 99: THE DOUBLOON

Ishmael returns to his shipmates, describing the reactions of Ahab, Starbuck, Stubb, Flask, the Manxman (a sailor from the Isle of Man, off the coast of England), Queequeg, Fedallah, and Pip to the golden coin fixed on the mainmast. The doubloon features a picture of three mountain peaks, one topped by a flame, one by a tower, and one by a rooster. Above the mountains, the sky is divided into a segment of the zodiac, with the sun entering the constellation Libra. Ahab remarks that the round coin is like the world in that man can see himself in it. Starbuck interprets it as a Christian symbol. Stubb, who had thought of the coin only as money to be spent, looks deeper at the doubloon after seeing his two superiors gaze meaningfully at it. Consulting his almanac to identify the zodiacal symbols, Stubb reflects that such books supply only bare facts, whereas people supply the thoughts that make facts meaningful.

He proceeds to interpret the entire zodiac as an allegory for the life of man. Flask sees only the monetary value of the coin and cannot understand what all of the staring has been about. The Manxman concludes that the ship will encounter the White Whale in a month and a day, when the sun is in the section of the zodiac depicted on the coin. Queequeg compares the coin to a tattoo on his leg but says nothing, while Fedallah makes a sign of reverence to the coin, perhaps because he is a sun worshipper. Pip looks last and says, portentously, that the coin is the ship's "navel"—the thing at the center of the ship that holds it together.

CHAPTER 100: LEG AND ARM: THE PEQUOD, OF NANTUCKET, MEETS THE SAMUEL ENDERBY, OF LONDON

The *Pequod* meets the *Samuel Enderby,* a whaling ship from London with a jolly captain and crew. Ahab asks if the other crew has encountered Moby Dick. The captain, named Boomer, has, and he lacks an arm because of it. The two mutilated captains touch their false limbs in a toast. The account of Boomer's lost arm is gory, but Boomer doesn't dwell too much on the horrible details, choosing instead to talk about the hot rum toddies that he drank during his recovery. From the little that he says, the *Pequod* men gather that Boomer was injured by a loose harpoon dangling from a line attached to Moby Dick. His arm was not severed but was amputated when the wound became gangrenous. The ship encountered the White Whale again, but, having learned his lesson, Boomer didn't try to hunt it a second time. Ahab insists on knowing which way the whale went; the *Samuel Enderby*'s crew believes him crazy. Refusing the other crew's hospitality, Ahab abruptly returns to his ship.

CHAPTER 101: THE DECANTER

Ishmael explains the significance of the name Samuel Enderby: this man fitted the first English sperm whaling ship. Ishmael is careful to point out that Americans had already been sperm-whaling for some time when the English got into the industry. He then offers some of the history behind the Enderby name before telling the story of the particular whaler *Samuel Enderby.* This and other British ships are well known for their hospitality, particularly in the way of alcoholic beverages.

ANALYSIS: CHAPTERS 93–101

The chapters in this section present a bewildering array of materials. The section is framed by the stories of Pip and Captain Boomer, each of whom undergoes a trauma at sea and responds to that trauma in his own way. Boomer's acceptance of his mutilation provides a sharp contrast to Ahab's furious thirst for vengeance. Indeed, the fellowship and good cheer represented by the *Samuel Enderby,* as well as its crew's unwillingness to pursue a hopeless and fatal quest, suggest a much more appealing way of going through life than the monomaniacal pursuit of a single goal represented by Ahab and the *Pequod.*

The chapters in which Ishmael describes the processing of the whale's body contribute to the reader's factual understanding of the ship's activities and purpose; more important, however, these activities provide the material upon which Ishmael exercises his imaginative and speculative faculties. His rhapsody about the pleasures of kneading the sperm with his fellow sailors is particularly striking, both for its obvious homoeroticism and for the remarkable conclusion that he draws from it. Life experience has gradually taught him that human beings cannot make themselves happy by pursuing vague or abstract goals, that they always have to shift their goals to pursue something concrete: a spouse, the pleasures of bed, the comfort of the fireside, the beauty of the countryside. With this outlook, Ishmael realizes that the pleasures of squeezing sperm with the other sailors are as real and perfect as any happiness in life.

The doubloon chapter makes a number of startling points about how people interpret the world. Ahab asserts that whether they look at a symbol or the entire world, they see a reflection of themselves. His statements that the firm tower, fiery volcano, and courageous fowl are all Ahab is thus self-consciously ironic—he knows that he projects himself onto the symbol. But this realization does not lead Ahab to examine himself critically as he examines the design on the coin. Instead, Ahab seems to conclude that people are simply trapped, unable to see anything but themselves, and thus can never grow or change.

The other sailors' comments on the coin bear out Ahab's point. Starbuck sees the coin as an emblem of the world that he sees around him: a vale of death, in which God, represented by the sun, offers a beacon of hope but no certainty. Stubb insightfully points out that human imagination must supply much of the meaning of any symbol, and, on seeing the zodiac apparently for the first time, he constructs a dazzling interpretation of the zodiacal signs as representing the twelve stages of a person's life. The picture of human life that results is typical of Stubb's fatalistic yet comical outlook.

CHAPTERS 102–114

CHAPTER 102: A BOWER IN THE ARSACIDES

Ishmael tries to understand the whale by measuring its bones. In an effort to bolster his credibility in describing the whale, he tells of a visit to his friend Tranquo, king of Tranque (apparently a fictional place). In Tranque, a large sperm whale skeleton is used as a temple, with its skull as an altar. Although the priests protested, claiming that it is impossible to measure God, Ishmael took the whale's dimensions and had them tattooed on his right arm. He had the dimensions recorded in short form because he wished to save as much space on his body as possible for "a blank page for a poem [he] was then composing."

CHAPTER 103: MEASUREMENT OF THE WHALE'S SKELETON

Ishmael offers his findings, based on the skeleton of the whale that he measured in Tranque. He believes that the largest sperm whales are around ninety tons, and "would considerably outweigh the combined population of a whole village of one thousand one hundred inhabitants." He then gives detailed dimensions of all parts of the whale's skeleton. These bones, he cautions, give only a partial picture of the whale, since so much flesh is wrapped around them and they don't capture the essence of the living animal. He adds that a person cannot find a good representation of a whale in its entirety.

CHAPTER 104: THE FOSSIL WHALE

Ishmael admits that he is "manhandling" the whale in his description, but he says that he is doing the best that he knows how. He decides to look at the Fossil Whale from an "archaeological, fossiliferous, and antediluvian point of view." He states that it is impossible for him to exaggerate with the words that he uses to describe the whale because the whale itself is so grand. He establishes his credentials as a geologist and presents his findings. Once again, he is unsatisfied with the picture of the whale that he has created: "the skeleton of the whale furnishes but little clue to the shape of his fully invested body." This chapter gives a sense of the whale's age as a species and his pedigree, and allows Ishmael to meditate on time as a construct of man.

CHAPTER 105: DOES THE WHALE'S MAGNITUDE DIMINISH? — WILL HE PERISH?

In awe of his subject, Ishmael finally admits defeat in his attempts to capture the whale through description. Now he questions whether such a fabulous monster will remain on the earth and if, as reports have it, its size is diminishing over time. Based on the fact that man and other animals have actually gotten larger throughout history, Ishmael believes that it is not likely that the whale has diminished in size. As for the whale's continued survival, Ishmael says that though whales may not travel in herds anymore and though their haunts may have changed, they remain nonetheless. He believes that their survival owes to the new home base they have established at the poles, where man cannot penetrate. He also notes that other large mammals have been extensively hunted and that the whale population is likely not in danger because it has an enormous home environment and because many generations of whales are alive at the same time. In fact, whales are particularly likely to endure—if there is another Noah's flood, Ishmael remarks, whales will not drown.

CHAPTER 106: AHAB'S LEG

Ahab asks the carpenter to make him a new leg, as the one that he uses is not trustworthy. After hitting it heavily on the boat's wooden floor when he returned from the *Samuel Enderby,* Ahab feels that his leg won't continue to hold together. Indeed, just before the *Pequod* sailed from Nantucket, Ishmael relates, Ahab had been found lying on the ground with the whalebone leg twisted around and almost piercing his groin.

CHAPTER 107: THE CARPENTER

The carpenter, the do-it-all man on the ship, has to make Ahab a new prosthetic leg. The carpenter is an able man, but he views everything, even parts of the human body, as pieces of a machine.

CHAPTER 108: AHAB AND THE CARPENTER: THE DECK— FIRST NIGHT WATCH

In this playlike scene, Ahab approaches the carpenter to be fitted for his new leg. He abuses the carpenter and discourses on hell and the feeling of a ghost leg. When Ahab leaves, the carpenter muses on the captain's queerness.

CHAPTER 109: AHAB AND STARBUCK IN THE CABIN

Sailors discover that the oil casks in the hold are leaking. Starbuck informs Ahab and suggests that they stop to fix them, but Ahab refuses to stop, saying that he doesn't care about the owners or profit. Starbuck objects, and Ahab points a musket at him. Says Starbuck, "I ask thee not to beware of Starbuck; thou wouldst but laugh; but let Ahab beware of Ahab; beware of thyself, old man." After Starbuck departs, Ahab abruptly gives in and orders the casks repaired. Ishmael speculates that Ahab's decision was a "prudential policy" to avoid angering the crew.

CHAPTER 110: QUEEQUEG IN HIS COFFIN

While the repairs are being made to the casks, Queequeg falls ill. Thinking he is going to die, he orders a coffin made and fills it with his harpoon, his idol, and various other important possessions. He lies in it and closes the cover, and Pip dances around the coffin. Pip asks Queequeg to look for the former's old, sane self in paradise after he dies. Queequeg soon feels well again and emerges from his coffin. Ishmael attributes this recovery to Queequeg's "savage" nature—Queequeg claims that he has willed himself back to health. Queequeg uses the coffin as a chest for his belongings and sets about copying the tattoos on his body onto the lid of the coffin. The tattoos were done by a prophet among his people and are supposed to depict "a complete theory of the heavens and the earth, and a mystical treatise on the art of attaining truth."

CHAPTER 111: THE PACIFIC
Ishmael ponders the meditative, serene Pacific Ocean. The sea promotes dreaminess and seems like heaven to him. Ishmael considers Ahab, noting that no such calming thoughts stir the captain's brain.

CHAPTER 112: THE BLACKSMITH
Ishmael then describes the *Pequod*'s blacksmith, whose life on land disintegrated after he turned to drink. Echoing his own initial reasons for shipping aboard the *Pequod,* Ishmael explains that the sea beckons to brokenhearted men who long for death but cannot commit suicide.

CHAPTER 113: THE FORGE
Ahab asks the blacksmith to make a special harpoon with which to kill the White Whale. He gives the blacksmith the stubs of the nails of racehorse shoes, the toughest steel known, with which to make the weapon. Although Ahab gives the blacksmith directions, he soon takes over the crafting of the harpoon himself, hammering the steel on the anvil and tempering it with the blood of the three harpooners instead of water. The scene ends with Pip's laughter ringing through the ship.

CHAPTER 114: THE GILDER
The dreaminess of the sea masks its ferocity. Ishmael speaks of the sea as "gilt" because it looks golden in the sunset and is falsely calm. The soothing scene inspires Ahab, Starbuck, and Stubbs to address the sea philosophically, each in his characteristic way.

ANALYSIS: CHAPTERS 102–114
In the first four chapters in this section, Ishmael continues to search for a way to represent the whale in its totality. He also becomes

more concerned with conceptualizing what he does as a writer and what gives his words authority. Just as the Tranque priests claim that God cannot be measured, Ishmael proves that the whale cannot be comprehended in its totality by means of an empirical description of its parts. However, such partial details are all that a writer has to work with.

Ishmael establishes his authority to write about the skeletons and fossil history of whales by recounting his trip to Tranque and his work as a stonemason and trench-digger. While these credentials are clearly ridiculous—Tranque is fictional, and a trench-digger cannot claim to be an expert on fossils—they point to his growing attention to the task of writing. In Chapter 85, Ishmael refers to the writer as a "profound being" who has little to say to the world but is "forced to stammer out something by way of getting a living." But in later chapters he seems unsure of his own profundity, focusing instead on experience as the source of narrative. He explains his own choice of tone and diction as expanding to fit his subject—the whale—which is both physically and symbolically enormous.

In Ishmael's narrative, tattoos combine writing and experience in unexpected ways. The measurements tattooed on his arm make Ishmael's body a living record of his experience. Moreover, he speaks of his plan to tattoo a much longer document on his body at some point in the future. Tattooing, as mentioned earlier, was seen in the nineteenth century as an irreversible mark of difference, testifying to an individual's separation from conventional white society. Ishmael's tattoos serve as a reminder that he has had experiences very different from those of a typical white man. Queequeg's tattoos also function as a record of experience and knowledge. They depict his culture's understanding of the universe and truth. Tradition and learning are passed on from person to person, and every person is a book, albeit in not quite so literal a fashion as Queequeg. Having no one from his home to whom he can pass on the knowledge inscribed on his body, Queequeg copies his tattoos onto his coffin, the symbol of his inevitable death. Appropriately, the coffin survives to the end of the novel, enabling the information carved on its lid to survive as well, just as the novel that Ishmael writes will survive his eventual death.

In these chapters, scenes of high drama alternate with scenes of tranquility and dreamlike peace. As earlier, some of these chapters are written as if they were scenes from a play. Dialogues, soliloquies, and asides are used with increasing frequency, which reminds the reader that Ahab is concocting his own drama and that the quest for Moby Dick is as artificial as a play. The alternation of dreamy contemplation with dramatic tension reflects the reality of whaling: the excitement of the hunt is tempered by long periods of watching and waiting.

CHAPTERS 115–125

CHAPTER 115: THE PEQUOD MEETS THE BACHELOR

The somber *Pequod*, still on the lookout for Moby Dick, encounters the *Bachelor*, a festive Nantucket whaler on its way home with a full cargo. The captain of the *Bachelor*, saying that he has heard stories of the White Whale but doesn't believe them, invites Ahab and the crew to join his party. Ahab declines, and the two ships go their separate ways as Ahab contemplates a vial of Nantucket sand that he has been carrying in his pocket.

CHAPTER 116: THE DYING WHALE

The next day, the *Pequod* kills several whales, and the way that one dying whale turns toward the sun inspires Ahab to speak to it in wondrous tones. He notes that the whale, like man, worships the sun's warmth. Ahab then hails the sea, calling its waves his "foster-brothers."

CHAPTER 117: THE WHALE WATCH

While keeping a night vigil over a whale that was too far away to take back to the ship immediately, Ahab hears from Fedallah the prophecy of his death. Before Ahab can die, he must see two hearses, one "not made by mortal hands" and one made of wood from America. Since it is unlikely that a hearse would be seen at sea, Ahab believes that he will not be killed on this voyage. Fedallah also tells him that he, Fedallah, will die before Ahab, and that only hemp can kill the captain. Ahab takes the latter prophecy to mean that he will be hanged, and again thinks his death unlikely to happen at sea.

CHAPTER 118: THE QUADRANT

Back on the ship, Ahab holds up a quadrant, an instrument that gauges the position of the sun, to determine the ship's latitude. Deciding that it doesn't give him the information that he wants, he tramples it underfoot. He orders the ship to change direction. Starbuck finds Ahab's ambitions petty and thinks that his behavior will end in mediocrity and failure. Stubb, on the other hand, respects Ahab for his willingness to "live in the game, and die in it!"

CHAPTER 119: THE CANDLES

The next day, the *Pequod* is caught in a typhoon, and one of the harpoon boats is destroyed. The weird weather makes white flames appear at the top of the three masts, but Ahab refuses to let the crew put up lightning rods to draw away the danger. While Ahab marvels at the ship's three masts lit up like three spermaceti candles, hailing them as good omens and signs of his own power, Starbuck sees them as a warning against continuing the quest for Moby Dick. When Starbuck sees Ahab's harpoon also flickering with fire, he interprets it as a sign that God opposes Ahab. Ahab, however, grasps the harpoon and says, in front of a frightened crew, that there is nothing to fear in the enterprise that binds them all together. He blows out the flame to "blow out the last fear."

CHAPTER 120: THE DECK TOWARDS THE END OF THE FIRST NIGHT WATCH

In the next chapter, Starbuck questions Ahab's judgment again, this time concerning the sails during the storm. Starbuck wants to take one of them down, but Ahab says that they should just lash it tighter. He complains that his first mate seems to think him incompetent.

CHAPTER 121: MIDNIGHT—THE FORECASTLE BULWARKS

Stubb and Flask have their own conversation about the storm and Ahab's behavior. Stubb dominates the conversation and insists that this journey is no more dangerous than any other, even though it seems as if Ahab is putting them in extreme danger.

CHAPTER 122: MIDNIGHT ALOFT—THUNDER AND LIGHTNING

Suspended above the men on the main-top-sail yard, Tashtego thinks to himself that sailors care more about rum than about the storm.

CHAPTER 123: THE MUSKET

When the storm finally dies down, Starbuck goes below to report to Ahab. On the way to the cabin, he sees a row of muskets, including the very one that Ahab had leveled at him earlier. Angry about Ahab's reckless and selfish behavior, he debates with himself about whether he ought to kill his captain. He decides that he cannot kill Ahab in his sleep and returns to the deck, asking Stubb to wake Ahab.

CHAPTER 124: THE NEEDLE

When Ahab is on deck the next day, he realizes that the storm has thrown off the compasses. He then pronounces himself "lord over the level loadstone yet" and makes his own needle. Here Ishmael notes that "[i]n this fiery eye of scorn and triumph, you then saw Ahab in all his fatal pride."

CHAPTER 125: THE LOG AND LINE
With all of the other orienting devices out of order, Ahab decides to pull out the seldom-used log and line, a device used to measure a ship's speed. Because of heat and moisture, the line breaks, and Ahab realizes that he now has none of his original navigational devices. He calls for Pip to help him, but Pip answers with nonsense. Ahab, touched by Pip's crazy speeches, says that his cabin will now be Pip's, because the boy touches his "inmost center."

ANALYSIS: CHAPTERS 115–125
Ishmael fades in and out of his own narration in these chapters, as Ahab's determination and control over the ship increase. Many of these chapters, in fact, are made up entirely of soliloquies and asides, for which it seems unlikely that Ishmael would have been an audience. The events that occur in these chapters also reflect Ahab's increasing power over the ship. First Ahab throws away the quadrant. He then refuses to put up the lightning rods, makes his own compass, and breaks the log and line. These devices are the only things that keep the *Pequod* on an objective, standard course. The loss of the ship's compass is probably most significant—its replacement with one of Ahab's own manufacture suggests that the *Pequod*'s path will now be dictated not by logic, skill, or convention but solely by Ahab's will.

Ahab has become so self-confident that he alters the prophecy delivered by Fedallah, his own private prophet, in order to make it conform to his own vision. For every part of Fedallah's prophecy, Ahab finds a reason that it will not apply to him. He assumes, for instance, that Fedallah's assertion that only hemp can cause Ahab's death means that he is to be hung. Ahab ignores the fact that he is on a ship hung with ropes, which are used in every aspect of sailing and whaling. Ishmael even frequently notes the sort of fatal accidents involving rope that can occur. Ahab's willful misreading of Fedallah's words demonstrates his hubris, or arrogant overconfidence.

Ahab acquires an unexpected double in the person of Pip. Pip and Ahab complement each other in many ways: Ahab is white, while Pip is black; Ahab is at the center of the intrigue, while Pip is marginal; Ahab is atop the shipboard hierarchy, while Pip is at the bottom; Ahab is old and wise, while Pip is young and knows nothing about whaling technique. Most important, however, Ahab seems to possess a modicum of sanity, while Pip seems to have crossed the line into insanity. Despite these differences, both see the world slightly aslant and feel alienated from the majority of the men on the ship. Their situation, as Pip explains it, creates between them a "man-rope; something that weak souls may hold by." Pip pulls at the deeply buried remnants of Ahab's humanity, and Ahab takes Pip almost as a son.

A crucial difference between Pip and Ahab is that Pip's insanity results from his coming to understand his own insignificance, both as a black man in white America and as one tiny human in the vast ocean. Ahab, on the other hand, feels himself to have been singled out by, rather than lost in, the vastness of the universe. Pip and Ahab thus represent two opposite psychological extremes.

The conflict between Starbuck and Ahab intensifies in these chapters as Starbuck questions the captain in front of the crew. The two men view the world in different ways, and their differences bring them into collision. Starbuck thinks about home with tenderness, considers the crew, and reasons rather than emotes. His indecision over whether to kill the sleeping Ahab and his thinking aloud recall the scene in *Hamlet* in which Hamlet vacillates about whether to kill Claudius, his father's murderer, while Claudius is praying.

CHAPTERS 126–132

CHAPTER 126: THE LIFE-BUOY

As the *Pequod* approaches the equatorial fishing ground, the sailors think that they hear mermaids or ghosts wailing. The Manxman says that these are the voices of the newly drowned men in the sea. Ahab laughs at this nonsense, telling the men that they have passed a seal colony in the night. Many of the men are superstitious about seals, though, and Ahab's explanation helps little. The next morning, one of the *Pequod*'s crew falls from a masthead. The life buoy that is thrown in after him is old and dried out, and it fills with water and sinks. The man drowns. Starbuck, Stubb, and Flask decide to replace the life buoy with Queequeg's coffin.

CHAPTER 127: THE DECK

This chapter is written in the form of a theatrical dialogue followed by a long soliloquy from Ahab. The carpenter grumbles about having to transform the coffin into a buoy. Ahab, aware of the irony of the substitution, calls the carpenter "unprincipled as the gods" for going through with it. He calls Pip to him to discuss the "wondrous philosophies" of the situation: since Pip's experience in the ocean, the two have been close companions.

CHAPTER 128: THE PEQUOD MEETS THE RACHEL
The *Pequod,* still looking for Moby Dick, encounters the *Rachel.* Captain Gardiner of the *Rachel,* after affirming that he has indeed seen Moby Dick, climbs aboard Ahab's ship and begs Ahab to help him find his son, whose whale boat was lost in the chase after the White Whale. Ahab refuses, not wanting to waste time that could be used in pursuit of Moby Dick.

CHAPTER 129: THE CABIN
Now that Ahab knows that Moby Dick is near, he spends much of his time walking the decks. One night, Pip tries to follow him, telling Ahab that he won't abandon him. Ahab tells Pip to stay in the captain's cabin, lest Pip's insanity cause Ahab's compassion for the boy to distract him from his lust for revenge.

CHAPTER 130: THE HAT
Ahab, shadowed everywhere by Fedallah, remains on deck, ever watchful. The crew falls into a routine of stifled silence. This continuous watch sharpens Ahab's obsession, and he decides that he must be the first to sight the whale. He asks Starbuck to help him get up the main-mast and watch his rope. While Ahab is up there, a black hawk steals his hat, which Ishmael considers a bad omen.

CHAPTER 131: THE PEQUOD MEETS THE DELIGHT
The *Pequod* then runs into the miserably misnamed *Delight,* which has previously encountered Moby Dick, with the unpleasant result of a gutted whale boat and dead men. As the *Pequod* goes by, the *Delight* drops a corpse in the water. The *Delight's* crew remarks upon the coffin life buoy at the *Pequod's* stern: to them, it is clear that the coffin is a symbol of doom.

CHAPTER 132: THE SYMPHONY
Ahab and Starbuck exchange stories about their wives and children, and Ahab talks sadly about his wearying quest for Moby Dick. He calls himself a fool and thinks himself pathetic. Starbuck suggests that he give up the chase, but Ahab doubts that he can stop, feeling impelled by fate. As Ahab debates this profound dilemma, Starbuck

steals away in despair. When Ahab goes to the other side of the deck to gaze into the water, Fedallah, too, looks over the rail.

ANALYSIS: CHAPTERS 126–132

This set of chapters prepares the reader and the *Pequod*'s crew for the final confrontation with Moby Dick. The atmosphere of doom and the feelings of inevitability grow stronger as the narrative progresses. The sailors, and probably the reader as well, are confused as to which events represent the fulfillment of prophecies of catastrophe and which are in themselves prophecies of disasters to come. The operation of fate and causality is thus unclear, and the justification for Ahab's quest comes to seem strained, as it becomes increasingly apparent, especially in the episodes with the *Rachel* and the *Delight,* that an encounter with Moby Dick is both fated and sure to be fatal. Given that the conclusion seems inevitable, events and objects such as the *Pequod*'s "baptism" as it is splashed by the corpse thrown from the *Delight,* or the coffin attached to the *Pequod*'s stern, take on significance as symbols rather than as causes.

Much has changed aboard the *Pequod* since the beginning of its voyage; most notable is that its power structure has been subverted. Pip, formerly a minor character, is now sitting "in the ship's full middle." Ahab, in fact, tells Pip to sit in his chair as if Pip "were the captain." Pip finds it strange that "a black boy [should play] host to white men with gold lace upon their coats!" He knows that people like him—the young, the black—typically serve older white men like Ahab. It is not clear whether Ahab is in complete control anymore. He asks himself:

> *What is it, what nameless, inscrutable, unearthly thing*
> *is it; what cozening, hidden lord and master, and cruel,*
> *remorseless emperor commands me; that against*
> *all natural lovings and longings, I so keep pushing,*
> *and crowding, and jamming myself on all the time;*
> *recklessly making me ready to do what in my own*
> *proper, natural heart, I durst not so much as dare? Is*
> *Ahab, Ahab?*

In this self-conscious moment, a rare instance of questioning his obsession, Ahab wonders about his free will and his identity. He understands both the folly of his quest and the fact that he is compelled to pursue it by some force that he cannot overcome.

CHAPTER 133–EPILOGUE

CHAPTER 133: THE CHASE—FIRST DAY

Ahab can sense by the smell of a whale in the air that Moby Dick is near. Climbing up to the main royal-mast, Ahab spots Moby Dick and earns himself the doubloon. All of the boats set off in chase of the whale. When Moby Dick finally surfaces, he does so directly beneath Ahab's boat, destroying it and casting its crew into the water. The whale threatens the men, but the *Pequod*, with Starbuck at the helm, drives it away, and the men are rescued by the other boats. The whale then moves away from the ship at a rapid rate, and the boats return to the ship. The men keep watch for Moby Dick, despite the misgivings of Starbuck and others.

CHAPTER 134: THE CHASE—SECOND DAY

Ishmael notes that it is not unprecedented for whalers to give extended pursuit to a particular whale. Ahab, despite the previous day's loss of the boat, is intent on the chase. They do sight Moby Dick again, and the crewmen, in awe of Ahab's wild power and caught up in the thrill, lower three boats. Starbuck again remains on board the *Pequod*. Ahab tries to attack Moby Dick head on this time, but again the whale is triumphant. Despite the harpoons in his side, he destroys the boats carrying Flask and Stubb by dashing them against one another. He also nearly kills Ahab's crew with the tangle of harpoons and lances caught in the line coming from his side. Ahab manages to cut and then reattach the line, removing the cluster of weapons.

Moby Dick then capsizes Ahab's boat. Ahab's whale-bone leg is snapped off in the mishap, and Ahab curses his body's weakness. Upon returning to the Pequod, Ahab finds out that Fedallah has drowned, dragged down by Ahab's own line, fulfilling one element of Fedallah's prophecy concerning Ahab's death—that Ahab would die after Fedallah. Starbuck begs Ahab to desist, but Ahab, convinced that he is only the "Fates' lieutenant," responds that he must continue to pursue the whale. The carpenter hastily makes Ahab a new leg from the remnants of his harpoon boat.

CHAPTER 135: THE CHASE — THIRD DAY

Towards thee I roll, thou all-destroying but
unconquering whale; to the last I grapple with thee;
from hell's heart I stab at thee.

(See QUOTATIONS, p. 78)

The crew seeks the White Whale for a third time but sees nothing until Ahab realizes, "Aye, he's chasing me now; not I, him—that's bad." They turn the ship around completely, and Ahab mounts the masthead himself. He sights the spout and comes back down to the deck again. As he gets into his boat and leaves Starbuck in charge, the two men exchange a poignant moment in which Ahab asks to shake hands with his first mate and the first mate tries to tell him not to go. Sharks bite at the oars as the boats pull away. Starbuck laments Ahab's certain doom. Ahab sees Moby Dick breach. The whale damages the other two boats, but Ahab's remains intact. Ahab sees Fedallah's corpse strapped to the whale by turns of rope and realizes that he is seeing the first hearse that Fedallah had predicted, in the sense that a hearse is a vehicle—here, the whale—that carries a corpse.

The whale goes down again, and Ahab rows close to the ship. He tells Tashtego to find another flag and nail it to the main masthead, as the Pequod's flag has somehow been removed from its usual spot. The boats sight the Moby Dick again and go after him. Moby Dick turns around and heads for the Pequod at full speed. He smashes the ship, which goes down without its captain. The ship, Ahab realizes, is the second hearse of Fedallah's prophecy, since it entombs its crew in "American" wood. Impassioned, Ahab is now determined to strike at Moby Dick with all of his power. After darting the whale, Ahab is caught around the neck by the flying line and dragged under the sea—the final element of Fedallah's prophesy. Tashtego, meanwhile, still tries to nail the flag to the ship's spar as it goes down. He catches a sky-hawk in mid-hammer, and the screaming bird, folded in the flag, goes down with everything else. The vortex from the sinking Pequod pulls the remaining harpoon boats and crew down with it.

EPILOGUE

Ishmael is the only survivor of the Pequod's encounter with Moby Dick. He escapes only because he had been thrown clear of the area in the wreck of Ahab's harpoon boat. Queequeg's coffin bobs up and becomes Ishmael's life buoy. A day after the wreck, the Rachel saves Ishmael as she continues to search for her own lost crew.

ANALYSIS: CHAPTER 133–EPILOGUE

Ahab's long-awaited encounter with Moby Dick brings to mind the drawn-out, fantastic battle scenes of myth and epic. He has sought the whale for a full year, the traditional time span of an epic quest. He now battles the whale for three days, stopping each night to rearm himself and repair the day's damage. However, Ahab is fated to lose, and he knows it. The whale seems to toy with the audacious humans, as it surfaces directly beneath their boats and sends a cluster of tangled harpoons and lances whizzing dangerously close to the sailors. Like an annoyed god, the whale means to teach these humans a lesson; Ahab will be punished for his arrogance. By the morning of the third day, Ahab has come to an understanding of the forces that drive him. "Ahab never thinks," he says aloud, "he only feels, feels, feels; . . . to think's audacity. God only has that right and privilege." By framing his quest as an emotional rather than an intellectual one, Ahab admits his own irrationality. Revenge, justice, and other such lofty ideals can be sought only by divine powers; man is too limited in his knowledge and his clout to do much more than react to the world around him.

A fatalist to the last, Ahab doesn't flee the whale, although anyone with common sense surely would have sailed the *Pequod* out of the whale's range at top speed after the first day's defeats. Ahab's death should not be read as a suicide, though. To the obsessed captain, each encounter with the whale fulfills a part of the prophecies made concerning his ultimate end. By going forward with the fight, he completes a larger design and gives his life and death a greater significance than it would have had otherwise. Only figures of importance—heroes, gods, martyrs—have their deaths foretold. By committing himself to a struggle he cannot win, Ahab becomes the stuff of legend.

Ahab's death suggests itself as a metaphor for the human condition. Man, of limited knowledge and meager powers, lives and dies struggling against forces that he can neither understand nor conquer. By continuing to fight the whale even when defeat is imminent, Ahab acts out, in dramatic form, the fate of all men. His request that Tashtego nail a new flag to the mast of the sinking ship is a sign not of defiance but of recognition that to be mortal is to persevere in the face of certain defeat, and that such perseverance is the highest and most heroic accomplishment of man.

Ishmael survives by floating on Queequeg's coffin, which had been transformed into the *Pequod*'s life buoy. The coffin symbolizes not only resurrection but also the persistence of narratives. Queequeg has cheated death by inscribing his tattoos on the coffin. Ahab too has cheated death, in a sense, since he will continue to live on through Ishmael's narration. The conclusion of *Moby-Dick* is laced with such ironies, which are the matter of myth, for *Moby-Dick,* though it encompasses allegory, adventure, and many other genres, is more than anything a myth about the follies of man.

IMPORTANT QUOTATIONS EXPLAINED

1. How it is I know not; but there is no place like a bed for confidential disclosures between friends. Man and wife, they say, there open the very bottom of their souls to each other; and some old couples often lie and chat over old times till nearly morning. Thus, then, in our hearts' honeymoon, lay I and Queequeg—a cosy, loving pair.

This passage comes at the end of Chapter 10, when Ishmael is forced to share a bed with the tattooed "savage" Queequeg at the Spouter-Inn. At first horrified, Ishmael is quickly impressed by Queequeg's dignity and kindness. The homoerotic overtones of their sharing a bed and staying up much of the night smoking and talking suggests a profound, close bond born of mutual dependence and a world in which merit, rather than race or wealth, determines a man's status. The men aboard the *Pequod* are everything to one another, and the relationships between them are stronger and more meaningful than even that between man and wife. Ishmael's willingness to describe his relationship with Queequeg in such conjugal terms ("honeymoon") symbolizes his openness to new experiences and people.

2.   Come, Ahab's compliments to ye; come and see if ye can
     swerve me. Swerve me? ye cannot swerve me, else ye
     swerve yourselves! man has ye there. Swerve me? The path
     to my fixed purpose is laid with iron rails, whereon my
     soul is grooved to run. Over unsounded gorges, through
     the rifled hearts of mountains, under torrents' beds,
     unerringly I rush! Naught's an obstacle, naught's an angle
     to the iron way!

Ahab speaks these words in his soliloquy in Chapter 37, daring anyone to try to divert him from his purpose. Though he is defiant, he
is also accepting of his fate, asserting that he has no control over
his own behavior—he must run along the "iron rails" that have
been laid for him. The powerful rhetoric and strong imagery of this
passage are characteristic of Ahab's speech. He uses his skill with
language to persuade his crew to take part in his quest for vengeance, stirring them with suggestions of adventure ("unsounded
gorges," "rifled hearts of mountains") and inspiring confidence
through his apparent faith in himself as "unerring." Just as Ishmael
occasionally gets lost in digressions, Ahab occasionally gets lost in
language, repeating the phrase "swerve me" until it becomes almost
meaningless, merely a sound. His speeches thus become a kind of
poetry or music, stirring the listener with their form as much as their
content.

3.   All that most maddens and torments; all that stirs up the lees of things; all truth with malice in it; all that cracks the sinews and cakes the brain; all the subtle demonisms of life and thought; all evil, to crazy Ahab, were visibly personified, and made practically assailable in Moby Dick. He piled upon the whale's white hump the sum of all the general rage and hate felt by his whole race from Adam down; and then, as if his chest had been a mortar, he burst his hot heart's shell upon it.

This quote, from Chapter 41, is the existential heart of the book; appropriately, the chapter from which it comes shares its title with the White Whale and the novel itself. While many sailors aboard the *Pequod* use legends about particularly large and malevolent whales as a way to manage the fear and danger inherent in whaling, they do not take these legends literally. Ahab, on the other hand, believes that Moby Dick is evil incarnate, and pits himself and humanity in an epic, timeless struggle against the White Whale. His belief that killing Moby Dick will eradicate evil evidences his inability to understand things symbolically: he is too literal a reader of the world around him. Instead of interpreting the loss of his leg as a common consequence of his occupation and perhaps as a punishment for taking excessive risks, he sees it as evidence of evil cosmic forces persecuting him.

QUOTATIONS

4. There is a wisdom that is woe; but there is a woe that is madness. And there is a Catskill eagle in some souls that can alike dive down into the blackest gorges, and soar out of them again and become invisible in the sunny spaces. And even if he for ever flies within the gorge, that gorge is in the mountains; so that even in his lowest swoop the mountain eagle is still higher than other birds upon the plain, even though they soar.

This passage comes at the end of Chapter 96, as Ishmael snaps out of a hypnotic state brought on by staring into the fires of the try-works. The image that Ishmael conjures here is typical of his philosophical speculation and his habit of quickly turning from a very literal subject to its metaphorical implications. This passage is a warning against giving in to escapism—fantasy, daydreaming, suicide—and suggests that woe and madness can be profitable states for one with enough greatness of soul. For one who is intelligent and perceptive—whose soul is "in the mountains" and greater than the average person's—such states of mind provide a higher plane of existence than contentedness and sanity do for a normal person. In other words, Ahab may be insane and "for ever . . . within the gorge," but his inherent greatness makes even his destruction more important than the mere existence—the "soar[ing]"—of other, more banal individuals.

5.   Towards thee I roll, thou all-destroying but unconquering
      whale; to the last I grapple with thee; from hell's heart I
      stab at thee; for hate's sake I spit my last breath at thee.
      Sink all coffins and all hearses to one common pool! and
      since neither can be mine, let me then tow to pieces, while
      still chasing thee, though tied to thee, thou damned whale!
      Thus, I give up the spear!

Ahab utters these words—his last—after Moby Dick destroys the
Pequod, in Chapter 135. As the action picks up pace, the sense of
tragedy becomes heightened. These words, Shakespearean in tone,
are meant to match the dramatic nature of the situation in which
they are spoken. Ahab dies as he began, defiant but aware of his
fate. The whale is "all-destroying but unconquering": its victory has
been inevitable, but it has not defeated Ahab's spirit. In an ultimate
demonstration of defiance, Ahab uses his "last breath" to curse the
whale and fate. He is, spiritually, already in "hell's heart," and he
acquiesces to his own imminent death. This final climactic explo-
sion of eloquence and theatricality is followed by an overwhelming
silence, as the whale disappears and everything and everyone but
Ishmael is pulled below the ocean's surface.

KEY FACTS

FULL TITLE
Moby-Dick; or *The Whale*

AUTHOR
Herman Melville

TYPE OF WORK
Novel

GENRE
Epic, adventure story, quest tale, allegory, tragedy

LANGUAGE
English

TIME AND PLACE WRITTEN
Between 1850 and 1851, in Pittsfield, Massachusetts, and New York City

DATE OF FIRST PUBLICATION
1851

PUBLISHER
Harper & Brothers in America (simultaneously published in England by Richard Bentley as *The Whale*)

NARRATOR
Ishmael, a junior member of the *Pequod*'s crew, casts himself as the author, recounting the events of the voyage after he has acquired more experience and studied the whale extensively.

POINT OF VIEW
Ishmael narrates in a combination of first and third person, describing events as he saw them and providing his own thoughts. He presents the thoughts and feelings of the other characters only as an outside observer might infer them.

TONE
Ironic, celebratory, philosophical, dramatic, hyperbolic

TENSE
Past

SETTING (TIME)
1830s or 1840s

SETTING (PLACE)
Aboard the whaling ship the *Pequod,* in the Pacific, Atlantic, and Indian Oceans

MAJOR CONFLICT
Ahab dedicates his ship and crew to destroying Moby Dick, a white sperm whale, because he sees this whale as the living embodiment of all that is evil and malignant in the universe. By ignoring the physical dangers that this quest entails, setting himself against other men, and presuming to understand and fight evil on a cosmic scale, Ahab arrogantly defies the limitations imposed upon human beings.

RISING ACTION
Ahab announces his quest to the other sailors and nails the doubloon to the mast; the *Pequod* encounters various ships with news and stories about Moby Dick.

CLIMAX
In Chapter 132, "The Symphony," Ahab interrogates himself and his quest in front of Starbuck, and realizes that he does not have the will to turn aside from his purpose.

FALLING ACTION
The death of Ahab and the destruction of the *Pequod* by Moby Dick; Ishmael, the only survivor of the *Pequod*'s sinking, floats on a coffin and is rescued by another whaling ship, the *Rachel.*

THEMES
The limits of knowledge; the deceptiveness of fate; the exploitative nature of whaling

MOTIFS
Whiteness; surfaces and depths

SYMBOLS
The *Pequod* symbolizes doom; Moby Dick, on an objective level, symbolizes humankind's inability to understand the world; Queequeg's coffin symbolizes both life and death

FORESHADOWING

Foreshadowing in *Moby-Dick* is extensive and inescapable: everything from the *Pequod's* ornamentation to the behavior of schools of fish to the appearance of a giant squid is read as an omen of the eventual catastrophic encounter with Moby Dick.

Study Questions

1. MOBY-DICK *features several characters who seem insane. How does insanity relate to this story? How do these characters contrast with one another?*

Ishmael describes Ahab as mad in his narration, and it does indeed seem mad to try to fight the forces of nature or God. However, some of the other characters in the novel whom Ishmael labels insane—notably Pip and Gabriel—might be viewed as wise rather than crazy, thus calling into question the possibility of making a clear distinction between sanity and insanity. Gabriel, the prophet figure aboard the *Jeroboam,* behaves irrationally and makes a number of ridiculous-sounding predictions. If viewed in a certain light, however, his prophecies sound not like silly attempts to foresee the future but like cleverly phrased efforts to effect change aboard his ship. Gabriel's prophecies are aimed at gaining the crew just treatment from the ship's officers and at avoiding the danger that will come from trying to hunt Moby Dick. Like Ahab, he manipulates the crew's superstitions and religious beliefs in order to gather support. But whereas Ahab's obsession is monomaniacal and selfish, Gabriel's "madness" is a response to irrational and unjust behavior on the part of those who control his ship.

2. *Ishmael frequently refers to the relationships between men in terms normally used to describe heterosexual romantic relationships. What is the literal and symbolic importance of homoeroticism in* MOBY-DICK?

Ishmael and Queequeg are depicted in bed together several times and are frequently described as "married" or "wedded" to each other. When they wake in the Spouter-Inn, Queequeg has his arms around Ishmael in a seemingly conjugal embrace. Melville uses the vocabulary of love and marriage to suggest the strength and closeness of the bonds between men at sea. Marriage is one of the institutions upon which society on land is organized, but there are no women aboard the *Pequod*. Instead, the crew develops a bond based on mutual dependence: they need each other to stay alive and are thus literally "wedded" to one another. In the absence of other relationships, they become everything to one another—metaphorical parents, siblings, best friends, and lovers. The replacement of heterosexual relationships, so central to conventional society, with homoerotic ones also signals a rejection of other aspects of life on land, such as racism, economic stratification, and limited opportunities for social mobility. Queequeg, for example, is taken aboard the *Pequod* for his expert marksmanship, despite his nonwhite skin.

3. *Describe the playlike scenes interspersed throughout* MOBY-DICK. *What is the function of these scenes? In what ways do they differ from the rest of the narrative?*

These scenes fall into two major categories: dramatic dialogues among several characters and soliloquies from a single character, often Ahab. The latter capture moments that Ishmael, the narrator, could not possibly have witnessed. Ahab must maintain his composure and certainty in front of his crew; it is only in private that he can express doubt or regret. These scenes are used to build dramatic tension, as they would in a play: Ahab senses the approach of catastrophe, which his soliloquies communicate to the reader by voicing his feeling of doom. The dialogue scenes frequently alternate with chapters that contain digressions from the plot. (Ishmael's measurements of the whale's skeleton, for example.) In this context, they become very suspenseful, as the plot is advanced purely through the authentic-seeming speech interactions of the sailors. Finally, by hearkening back to well-known dramatic works, these dramatic scenes also remind the reader of *Moby-Dick*'s thematic connections to tragic drama, particularly Shakespeare.

How to Write
Literary Analysis

The Literary Essay: A Step-by-Step Guide

When you read for pleasure, your only goal is enjoyment. You might find yourself reading to get caught up in an exciting story, to learn about an interesting time or place, or just to pass time. Maybe you're looking for inspiration, guidance, or a reflection of your own life. There are as many different, valid ways of reading a book as there are books in the world.

When you read a work of literature in an English class, however, you're being asked to read in a special way: you're being asked to perform *literary analysis*. To analyze something means to break it down into smaller parts and then examine how those parts work, both individually and together. Literary analysis involves examining all the parts of a novel, play, short story, or poem—elements such as character, setting, tone, and imagery—and thinking about how the author uses those elements to create certain effects.

A literary essay isn't a book review: you're not being asked whether or not you liked a book or whether you'd recommend it to another reader. A literary essay also isn't like the kind of book report you wrote when you were younger, where your teacher wanted you to summarize the book's action. A high school- or college-level literary essay asks, "How does this piece of literature actually work?" "How does it do what it does?" and, "Why might the author have made the choices he or she did?"

The Seven Steps

No one is born knowing how to analyze literature; it's a skill you learn and a process you can master. As you gain more practice with this kind of thinking and writing, you'll be able to craft a method that works best for you. But until then, here are seven basic steps to writing a well-constructed literary essay:

1. *Ask questions*
2. *Collect evidence*
3. *Construct a thesis*

4. *Develop and organize arguments*
5. *Write the introduction*
6. *Write the body paragraphs*
7. *Write the conclusion*

1. ASK QUESTIONS

When you're assigned a literary essay in class, your teacher will often provide you with a list of writing prompts. Lucky you! Now all you have to do is choose one. Do yourself a favor and pick a topic that interests you. You'll have a much better (not to mention easier) time if you start off with something you enjoy thinking about. If you are asked to come up with a topic by yourself, though, you might start to feel a little panicked. Maybe you have too many ideas—or none at all. Don't worry. Take a deep breath and start by asking yourself these questions:

- **What struck you?** Did a particular image, line, or scene linger in your mind for a long time? If it fascinated you, chances are you can draw on it to write a fascinating essay.

- **What confused you?** Maybe you were surprised to see a character act in a certain way, or maybe you didn't understand why the book ended the way it did. Confusing moments in a work of literature are like a loose thread in a sweater: if you pull on it, you can unravel the entire thing. Ask yourself why the author chose to write about that character or scene the way he or she did and you might tap into some important insights about the work as a whole.

- **Did you notice any patterns?** Is there a phrase that the main character uses constantly or an image that repeats throughout the book? If you can figure out how that pattern weaves through the work and what the significance of that pattern is, you've almost got your entire essay mapped out.

- **Did you notice any contradictions or ironies?** Great works of literature are complex; great literary essays recognize and explain those complexities. Maybe the title (*Happy Days*) totally disagrees with the book's subject matter (hungry orphans dying in the woods). Maybe the main character acts one way around his family and a completely different way around his friends and associates. If you can find a way to explain a work's contradictory elements, you've got the seeds of a great essay.

At this point, you don't need to know exactly what you're going to say about your topic; you just need a place to begin your exploration. You can help direct your reading and brainstorming by formulating your topic as a *question,* which you'll then try to answer in your essay. The best questions invite critical debates and discussions, not just a rehashing of the summary. Remember, you're looking for something you can *prove or argue* based on evidence you find in the text. Finally, remember to keep the scope of your question in mind: is this a topic you can adequately address within the word or page limit you've been given? Conversely, is this a topic big enough to fill the required length?

GOOD QUESTIONS

"Are Romeo and Juliet's parents responsible for the deaths of their children?"

"Why do pigs keep showing up in LORD OF THE FLIES?"
"Are Dr. Frankenstein and his monster alike? How?"

BAD QUESTIONS

"What happens to Scout in TO KILL A MOCKINGBIRD?"
"What do the other characters in JULIUS CAESAR think about Caesar?"

"How does Hester Prynne in THE SCARLET LETTER remind me of my sister?"

---

2. COLLECT EVIDENCE

Once you know what question you want to answer, it's time to scour the book for things that will help you answer the question. Don't worry if you don't know what you want to say yet—right now you're just collecting ideas and material and letting it all percolate. Keep track of passages, symbols, images, or scenes that deal with your topic. Eventually, you'll start making connections between these examples and your thesis will emerge.

Here's a brief summary of the various parts that compose each and every work of literature. These are the elements that you will analyze in your essay, and which you will offer as evidence to support your arguments. For more on the parts of literary works, see the Glossary of Literary Terms at the end of this section.

ELEMENTS OF STORY   These are the *what*s of the work—what happens, where it happens, and to whom it happens.

- **Plot:** All of the events and actions of the work.

- **Character:** The people who act and are acted upon in a literary work. The main character of a work is known as the *protagonist.*

- **Conflict:** The central tension in the work. In most cases, the protagonist wants something, while opposing forces (antagonists) hinder the protagonist's progress.

- **Setting:** When and where the work takes place. Elements of setting include location, time period, time of day, weather, social atmosphere, and economic conditions.

- **Narrator:** The person telling the story. The narrator may straightforwardly report what happens, convey the subjective opinions and perceptions of one or more characters, or provide commentary and opinion in his or her own voice.

- **Themes:** The main idea or message of the work—usually an abstract idea about people, society, or life in general. A work may have many themes, which may be in tension with one another.

ELEMENTS OF STYLE   These are the *how*s—how the characters speak, how the story is constructed, and how language is used throughout the work.

- **Structure and organization:** How the parts of the work are assembled. Some novels are narrated in a linear, chronological fashion, while others skip around in time. Some plays follow a traditional three- or five-act structure, while others are a series of loosely connected scenes. Some authors deliberately leave gaps in their works, leaving readers to puzzle out the missing information. A work's structure and organization can tell you a lot about the kind of message it wants to convey.

- **Point of view:** The perspective from which a story is told. In *first-person point of view,* the narrator involves him or herself in the story. ("I went to the store"; "We watched in horror as the bird slammed into the window.") A first-person narrator is usually the protagonist of the work, but not always. In *third-person point of view,* the narrator does not participate in the story. A third-person narrator may closely follow a specific character, recounting that individual character's thoughts or experiences, or it may be what we call an *omniscient* narrator. Omniscient narrators see and know all: they can witness any event in any time or place and are privy to the inner thoughts and feelings of all characters. Remember that the narrator and the author are not the same thing!

- **Diction:** Word choice. Whether a character uses dry, clinical language or flowery prose with lots of exclamation points can tell you a lot about his or her attitude and personality.

- **Syntax:** Word order and sentence construction. Syntax is a crucial part of establishing an author's narrative voice. Ernest Hemingway, for example, is known for writing in very short, straightforward sentences, while James Joyce characteristically wrote in long, incredibly complicated lines.

- **Tone:** The mood or feeling of the text. Diction and syntax often contribute to the tone of a work. A novel written in short, clipped sentences that use small, simple words might feel brusque, cold, or matter-of-fact.

- **Imagery:** Language that appeals to the senses, representing things that can be seen, smelled, heard, tasted, or touched.

- **Figurative language:** Language that is not meant to be interpreted literally. The most common types of figurative language are *metaphors* and *similes,* which compare two unlike things in order to suggest a similarity between them— for example, "All the world's a stage," or "The moon is like a ball of green cheese." (Metaphors say one thing *is* another thing; similes claim that one thing is *like* another thing.)

---

3. CONSTRUCT A THESIS

When you've examined all the evidence you've collected and know how you want to answer the question, it's time to write your thesis statement. A *thesis* is a claim about a work of literature that needs to be supported by evidence and arguments. The thesis statement is the heart of the literary essay, and the bulk of your paper will be spent trying to prove this claim. A good thesis will be:

- **Arguable.** "*The Great Gatsby* describes New York society in the 1920s" isn't a thesis—it's a fact.

- **Provable through textual evidence**. "*Hamlet* is a confusing but ultimately very well-written play" is a weak thesis because it offers the writer's personal opinion about the book. Yes, it's arguable, but it's not a claim that can be proved or supported with examples taken from the play itself.

- **Surprising**. "Both George and Lenny change a great deal in *Of Mice and Men*" is a weak thesis because it's obvious. A really strong thesis will argue for a reading of the text that is not immediately apparent.

- **Specific**. "Dr. Frankenstein's monster tells us a lot about the human condition" is *almost* a really great thesis statement, but it's still too vague. What does the writer mean by "a lot"? *How* does the monster tell us so much about the human condition?

GOOD THESIS STATEMENTS

Question: In *Romeo and Juliet*, which is more powerful in shaping the lovers' story: fate or foolishness?

Thesis: "Though Shakespeare defines Romeo and Juliet as 'star-crossed lovers' and images of stars and planets appear throughout the play, a closer examination of that celestial imagery reveals that the stars are merely witnesses to the characters' foolish activities and not the causes themselves."

Question: How does the bell jar function as a symbol in Sylvia Plath's *The Bell Jar*?

Thesis: "A bell jar is a bell-shaped glass that has three basic uses: to hold a specimen for observation, to contain gases, and to maintain a vacuum. The bell jar appears in each of these capacities in *The Bell Jar*, Plath's semi-autobiographical novel, and each appearance marks a different stage in Esther's mental breakdown."

Question: Would Piggy in *The Lord of the Flies* make a good island leader if he were given the chance?

Thesis: "Though the intelligent, rational, and innovative Piggy has the mental characteristics of a good leader, he ultimately lacks the social skills necessary to be an effective one. Golding emphasizes this point by giving Piggy a foil in the charismatic Jack, whose magnetic personality allows him to capture and wield power effectively, if not always wisely."

LITERARY ANALYSIS

---

4. DEVELOP AND ORGANIZE ARGUMENTS

The reasons and examples that support your thesis will form the middle paragraphs of your essay. Since you can't really write your thesis statement until you know how you'll structure your argument, you'll probably end up working on steps 3 and 4 at the same time.

There's no single method of argumentation that will work in every context. One essay prompt might ask you to compare and contrast two characters, while another asks you to trace an image through a given work of literature. These questions require different kinds of answers and therefore different kinds of arguments. Below, we'll discuss three common kinds of essay prompts and some strategies for constructing a solid, well-argued case.

TYPES OF LITERARY ESSAYS

- **Compare and contrast**

  Compare and contrast the characters of Huck and Jim in THE ADVENTURES OF HUCKLEBERRY FINN.

  Chances are you've written this kind of essay before. In an academic literary context, you'll organize your arguments the same way you would in any other class. You can either go *subject by subject* or *point by point*. In the former, you'll discuss one character first and then the second. In the latter, you'll choose several traits (attitude toward life, social status, images and metaphors associated with the character) and devote a paragraph to each. You may want to use a mix of these two approaches—for example, you may want to spend a paragraph a piece broadly sketching Huck's and Jim's personalities before transitioning into a paragraph or two that describes a few key points of comparison. This can be a highly effective strategy if you want to make a counterintuitive argument—that, despite seeming to be totally different, the two objects being compared are actually similar in a very important way (or vice versa). Remember that your essay should reveal something fresh or unexpected about the text, so think beyond the obvious parallels and differences.

- **Trace**

  Choose an image—for example, birds, knives, or eyes—and trace that image throughout MACBETH.

Sounds pretty easy, right? All you need to do is read the play, underline every appearance of a knife in *Macbeth*, and then list them in your essay in the order they appear, right? Well, not exactly. Your teacher doesn't want a simple catalog of examples. He or she wants to see you make *connections* between those examples—that's the difference between summarizing and analyzing. In the *Macbeth* example above, think about the different contexts in which knives appear in the play and to what effect. In *Macbeth*, there are real knives and imagined knives; knives that kill and knives that simply threaten. Categorize and classify your examples to give them some order. Finally, always keep the overall effect in mind. After you choose and analyze your examples, you should come to some greater understanding about the work, as well as your chosen image, symbol, or phrase's role in developing the major themes and stylistic strategies of that work.

- **Debate**

  Is the society depicted in 1984 good for its citizens?

  In this kind of essay, you're being asked to debate a moral, ethical, or aesthetic issue regarding the work. You might be asked to judge a character or group of characters (*Is Caesar responsible for his own demise?*) or the work itself (*Is* JANE EYRE *a feminist novel?*). For this kind of essay, there are two important points to keep in mind. First, don't simply base your arguments on your personal feelings and reactions. Every literary essay expects you to read and analyze the work, so search for evidence in the text. What do characters in *1984* have to say about the government of Oceania? What images does Orwell use that might give you a hint about his attitude toward the government? As in any debate, you also need to make sure that you define all the necessary terms before you begin to argue your case. What does it mean to be a "good" society? What makes a novel "feminist"? You should define your terms right up front, in the first paragraph after your introduction.

  Second, remember that strong literary essays make contrary and surprising arguments. Try to think outside the box. In the *1984* example above, it seems like the obvious answer would be no, the totalitarian society depicted in Orwell's novel is *not* good for its citizens. But can you think of any arguments for the opposite side? Even if your final assertion is that the novel depicts a cruel, repressive, and therefore harmful society, acknowledging and responding to the counterargument will strengthen your overall case.

---

5. WRITE THE INTRODUCTION

Your introduction sets up the entire essay. It's where you present your topic and articulate the particular issues and questions you'll be addressing. It's also where you, as the writer, introduce yourself to your readers. A persuasive literary essay immediately establishes its writer as a knowledgeable, authoritative figure.

An introduction can vary in length depending on the overall length of the essay, but in a traditional five-paragraph essay it should be no longer than one paragraph. However long it is, your introduction needs to:

- **Provide any necessary context.** Your introduction should situate the reader and let him or her know what to expect. What book are you discussing? Which characters? What topic will you be addressing?

- **Answer the "So what?" question.** Why is this topic important, and why is your particular position on the topic noteworthy? Ideally, your introduction should pique the reader's interest by suggesting how your argument is surprising or otherwise counterintuitive. Literary essays make unexpected connections and reveal less-than-obvious truths.

- **Present your thesis.** This usually happens at or very near the end of your introduction.

- **Indicate the shape of the essay to come.** Your reader should finish reading your introduction with a good sense of the scope of your essay as well as the path you'll take toward proving your thesis. You don't need to spell out every step, but you do need to suggest the organizational pattern you'll be using.

Your introduction should not:

- **Be vague.** Beware of the two killer words in literary analysis: *interesting* and *important*. Of course the work, question, or example is interesting and important—that's why you're writing about it!

- **Open with any grandiose assertions.** Many student readers think that beginning their essays with a flamboyant statement such as, "Since the dawn of time, writers have been fascinated with the topic of free will," makes them sound important and commanding. You know what? It actually sounds pretty amateurish.

- **Wildly praise the work.** Another typical mistake student writers make is extolling the work or author. Your teacher doesn't need to be told that "Shakespeare is perhaps the greatest writer in the English language." You can mention a work's reputation in passing—by referring to *The Adventures of Huckleberry Finn* as "Mark Twain's enduring classic," for example—but don't make a point of bringing it up unless that reputation is key to your argument.

- **Go off-topic.** Keep your introduction streamlined and to the point. Don't feel the need to throw in all kinds of bells and whistles in order to impress your reader—just get to the point as quickly as you can, without skimping on any of the required steps.

---

6. WRITE THE BODY PARAGRAPHS

Once you've written your introduction, you'll take the arguments you developed in step 4 and turn them into your body paragraphs. The organization of this middle section of your essay will largely be determined by the argumentative strategy you use, but no matter how you arrange your thoughts, your body paragraphs need to do the following:

- **Begin with a strong topic sentence.** Topic sentences are like signs on a highway: they tell the reader where they are and where they're going. A good topic sentence not only alerts readers to what issue will be discussed in the following paragraph but also gives them a sense of what argument will be made *about* that issue. "Rumor and gossip play an important role in *The Crucible*" isn't a strong topic sentence because it doesn't tell us very much. "The community's constant gossiping creates an environment that allows false accusations to flourish" is a much stronger topic sentence— it not only tells us *what* the paragraph will discuss (gossip) but *how* the paragraph will discuss the topic (by showing how gossip creates a set of conditions that leads to the play's climactic action).

- **Fully and completely develop a single thought.** Don't skip around in your paragraph or try to stuff in too much material. Body paragraphs are like bricks: each individual one needs to be strong and sturdy or the entire structure will collapse. Make sure you have really proven your point before moving on to the next one.

- **Use transitions effectively.** Good literary essay writers know that each paragraph must be clearly and strongly linked to the material around it. Think of each paragraph as a response to the one that precedes it. Use transition words and phrases such as *however, similarly, on the contrary, therefore,* and *furthermore* to indicate what kind of response you're making.

---

7. WRITE THE CONCLUSION

Just as you used the introduction to ground your readers in the topic before providing your thesis, you'll use the conclusion to quickly summarize the specifics learned thus far and then hint at the broader implications of your topic. A good conclusion will:

- **Do more than simply restate the thesis.** If your thesis argued that *The Catcher in the Rye* can be read as a Christian allegory, don't simply end your essay by saying, "And that is why *The Catcher in the Rye* can be read as a Christian allegory." If you've constructed your arguments well, this kind of statement will just be redundant.

- **Synthesize the arguments, not summarize them.** Similarly, don't repeat the details of your body paragraphs in your conclusion. The reader has already read your essay, and chances are it's not so long that they've forgotten all your points by now.

- **Revisit the "So what?" question.** In your introduction, you made a case for why your topic and position are important. You should close your essay with the same sort of gesture. What do your readers know now that they didn't know before? How will that knowledge help them better appreciate or understand the work overall?

- **Move from the specific to the general.** Your essay has most likely treated a very specific element of the work—a single character, a small set of images, or a particular passage. In your conclusion, try to show how this narrow discussion has wider implications for the work overall. If your essay on *To Kill a Mockingbird* focused on the character of Boo Radley, for example, you might want to include a bit in your conclusion about how he fits into the novel's larger message about childhood, innocence, or family life.

- **Stay relevant.** Your conclusion should suggest new directions of thought, but it shouldn't be treated as an opportunity to pad your essay with all the extra, interesting ideas you came up with during your brainstorming sessions but couldn't fit into the essay proper. Don't attempt to stuff in unrelated queries or too many abstract thoughts.

- **Avoid making overblown closing statements.** A conclusion should open up your highly specific, focused discussion, but it should do so without drawing a sweeping lesson about life or human nature. Making such observations may be part of the point of reading, but it's almost always a mistake in essays, where these observations tend to sound overly dramatic or simply silly.

A+ Essay Checklist

Congratulations! If you've followed all the steps we've outlined above, you should have a solid literary essay to show for all your efforts. What if you've got your sights set on an A+? To write the kind of superlative essay that will be rewarded with a perfect grade, keep the following rubric in mind. These are the qualities that teachers expect to see in a truly A+ essay. How does yours stack up?

- ✓ Demonstrates a thorough understanding of the book
- ✓ Presents an original, compelling argument
- ✓ Thoughtfully analyzes the text's formal elements
- ✓ Uses appropriate and insightful examples
- ✓ Structures ideas in a logical and progressive order
- ✓ Demonstrates a mastery of sentence construction, transitions, grammar, spelling, and word choice

LITERARY ANALYSIS

SUGGESTED ESSAY TOPICS

1. *Why does Ishmael include so many digressions in his narrative? Why does he draw on so many other disciplines (geology, art, biology)? Choose one of these digressions (the chapter on "Cetology," for example) and discuss the ways in which it comments on the main narrative.*

2. *Describe Ishmael's method of narration. Is he reliable or unreliable as a narrator? Why is he the one to tell this story? What would the narrative have been like if Ahab were the narrator?*

3. *How is the concept of fate used to organize the narrative? Does fate justify Ahab's actions? What is the relationship between fate and prophecy? What does fate have to do with religion, particularly Christianity?*

4. *Explain some of the biblical references in* MOBY-DICK. *How does Melville use the Bible as a literary model and as a source for thematic material?*

A+ Student Essay

Analyze Ishmael's reluctance to share his bed with Queequeg. How do their early interactions reflect the novel's major themes?

One of the dramatic highpoints of *Moby-Dick,* a novel that involves whirlpools, madness, and a terrifying whale, is one man's simple decision to share a room with a stranger. By making this seemingly negligible gesture the focus of the first part of his sprawling novel, Melville suggests that life's greatest challenges include meeting and communicating honestly with new people. This basic act is also at the center of Father Mapple's retelling of the Jonah story, in which a man risks imprisonment and death at sea merely to shirk the responsibility of sharing God's word with others. The dread of communication also paralyses several of the New Bedford residents Ishmael observes, from adult churchgoers to hardened, courageous sailors. The crisis over Ishmael's rooming assignment thus introduces one of Melville's major themes: the difficulty of knowing another human being and the human habit of avoiding honest, vulnerable interactions.

By dwelling on Ishmael's ignorant worries about Queequeg, Melville dramatizes the common fear of befriending and conversing with a new person. Ishmael considers locking the harpooner out of his bedroom just so he, Ishmael, can avoid interacting with him. Ishmael indulges a series of baseless, prejudicial thoughts about Queequeg, from the suspicion that he'll wave decapitated heads at him to the prissy concern that his linens will not be clean or fine. Ishmael even sets out to sleep on two benches of differing heights to shrug off the burden of making a friend. Once he is forced to spend a night with Queequeg and begins to develop an interest in him, however, Ishmael observes that "ignorance is the parent of fear"—he had worked himself into a frenzy for the sole reason that he'd never met Queequeg. The protracted saga of the rooming arrangement reinforces Melville's idea that some men live in fear of one another, too shy to try to bridge the gaps of language or cultural background.

This sense of widespread anxiety colors Father Mapple's interpretation of the Jonah story, in which a man goes to incredible lengths to avoid talking with his fellow men. Afraid to preach God's word, Jonah becomes "self-condemning in his look," for it's easier for him to detest himself as a coward than to incur the risks of communication. Jonah lies to and even pays the captain of a ship to allow him to sail far away from his native land, because it's less frightening to face imprisonment than to preach love and tolerance to other people. A whale swallows and almost kills Jonah before he is willing to admit to God that he dreads his duties as prophet. Again, the anxiety of communication drives a character to ludicrous extremes in the first part of the novel.

Like Jonah, several of the characters Ishmael observes demonstrate the difficulty and pain of building a community and the terror of speaking honestly and vulnerably with one's neighbors. Having thought that courageous service on the high seas would make men eloquent and self-possessed, Ishmael is amazed at the timidity of the "whalemen" who sit together at the Spouter-Inn, united by a common passion yet unwilling to share their stories. Again, at church, he observes "each silent worshipper . . . purposely sitting apart from the other, as if each silent grief were insular and incommunicable." The worshippers could alleviate some of the anguish they're feeling by opening up to one another, but the effort is unendurable. Ishmael observes the strapping Bulkington isolated from his shipmates, unwilling to share in the pleasure of storytelling and laughter. Repeatedly, men and women succumb to the dread of revealing themselves to one another, the fear that communication will somehow wound, expose, or endanger them.

The hand wringing that precedes Ishmael's meeting with Queequeg thus reinforces Melville's interest in the difficulty of getting to know another person and the measures some men take to avoid meaningful interactions. Ishmael almost sacrifices several nights of sleep simply because he worries Queequeg will be an unpleasant bedfellow. Jonah sets himself on a course of destruction, merely to shirk the task of spreading God's word in his community. Mourners and whalemen sit in silence, far apart, for the pressure to communicate is too much for them to bear. Throughout the novel, Melville recalls Ishmael's concerns in his early scenes with Queequeg, emphasizing the courage it takes to have a simple, truthful exchange, dramatizing the anxieties and alienation of the Pequod's wounded men.

LITERARY ANALYSIS

GLOSSARY OF LITERARY TERMS

ANTAGONIST

The entity that acts to frustrate the goals of the *protagonist*. The antagonist is usually another *character* but may also be a non-human force.

ANTIHERO / ANTIHEROINE

A *protagonist* who is not admirable or who challenges notions of what should be considered admirable.

CHARACTER

A person, animal, or any other thing with a personality that appears in a *narrative*.

CLIMAX

The moment of greatest intensity in a text or the major turning point in the *plot*.

CONFLICT

The central struggle that moves the *plot* forward. The conflict can be the *protagonist*'s struggle against fate, nature, society, or another person.

FIRST-PERSON POINT OF VIEW

A literary style in which the *narrator* tells the story from his or her own *point of view* and refers to himself or herself as "I." The narrator may be an active participant in the story or just an observer.

HERO / HEROINE

The principal *character* in a literary work or *narrative*.

IMAGERY

Language that brings to mind sense-impressions, representing things that can be seen, smelled, heard, tasted, or touched.

MOTIF

A recurring idea, structure, contrast, or device that develops or informs the major *themes* of a work of literature.

NARRATIVE

A story.

LITERARY ANALYSIS

NARRATOR
> The person (sometimes a *character*) who tells a story; the *voice* assumed by the writer. The narrator and the author of the work of literature are not the same person.

PLOT
> The arrangement of the events in a story, including the sequence in which they are told, the relative emphasis they are given, and the causal connections between events.

POINT OF VIEW
> The *perspective* that a *narrative* takes toward the events it describes.

PROTAGONIST
> The main *character* around whom the story revolves.

SETTING
> The location of a *narrative* in time and space. Setting creates mood or atmosphere.

SUBPLOT
> A secondary *plot* that is of less importance to the overall story but may serve as a point of contrast or comparison to the main plot.

SYMBOL
> An object, *character,* figure, or color that is used to represent an abstract idea or concept. Unlike an *emblem*, a symbol may have different meanings in different contexts.

SYNTAX
> The way the words in a piece of writing are put together to form lines, phrases, or clauses; the basic structure of a piece of writing.

THEME
> A fundamental and universal idea explored in a literary work.

TONE
> The author's attitude toward the subject or *characters* of a story or poem or toward the reader.

VOICE
> An author's individual way of using language to reflect his or her own personality and attitudes. An author communicates voice through *tone, diction,* and *syntax*.

LITERARY ANALYSIS

A Note on Plagiarism

Plagiarism—presenting someone else's work as your own—rears its ugly head in many forms. Many students know that copying text without citing it is unacceptable. But some don't realize that even if you're not quoting directly, but instead are paraphrasing or summarizing, *it is plagiarism* unless you cite the source.

Here are the most common forms of plagiarism:

- Using an author's phrases, sentences, or paragraphs without citing the source
- Paraphrasing an author's ideas without citing the source
- Passing off another student's work as your own

How do you steer clear of plagiarism? You should *always* acknowledge all words and ideas that aren't your own by using quotation marks around verbatim text or citations like footnotes and endnotes to note another writer's ideas. For more information on how to give credit when credit is due, ask your teacher for guidance or visit www.sparknotes.com.

Review & Resources

Quiz

1. Where does Ishmael want to go to find a berth on a whaling ship?

   A. Boston
   B. Nantucket
   C. New Bedford
   D. New York

2. Which biblical figure is the focus of Father Mapple's sermon?

   A. Job
   B. Solomon
   C. Isaiah
   D. Jonah

3. Which body part has Ahab lost to Moby Dick?

   A. His leg
   B. His arm
   C. His eye
   D. His fingers

4. What is the name of Ahab's ship?

   A. The *Town-Ho*
   B. The *Rachel*
   C. The *Samuel Enderby*
   D. The *Pequod*

5. After what is Ahab's ship named?

   A. Its owner
   B. A vanished tribe of Native Americans
   C. A species of whale
   D. A biblical character

6. For what were whales primarily hunted?

   A. Oil
   B. Skin
   C. Meat
   D. Fins

7. Which of the following characters falls overboard and goes insane as a result?

   A. Tashtego
   B. Pip
   C. Queequeg
   D. Starbuck

8. Who rescues Tashtego when he falls overboard inside the whale's head?

   A. Ishmael
   B. Stubb
   C. Fedallah
   D. Queequeg

9. What does Ahab nail to the ship's mast to motivate his crew in his quest for Moby Dick?

   A. A gold coin
   B. A severed head
   C. A drawing of Moby Dick
   D. A pirate flag

10. Which of the following characters survives the *Pequod's* sinking?

   A. Pip
   B. Ahab
   C. Flask
   D. None of the above

11. What keeps Ishmael afloat after the *Pequod* sinks?

    A. A coffin
    B. A barrel of oil
    C. A lifeboat
    D. A mattress

12. What does the crew look for to indicate the presence of a whale?

    A. Fins
    B. Spouts
    C. Seabirds
    D. Lightning

13. What frightens Ishmael the most about Moby Dick?

    A. The whale's size
    B. The whale's teeth
    C. The whiteness of the whale
    D. The sounds that the whale makes

14. What is cetology?

    A. The skill of navigation
    B. The study of old manuscripts
    C. The process used to render oil out of a whale
    D. The study of whales

15. What covers Queequeg's skin?

    A. Scars
    B. Tattoos
    C. Hair
    D. Blisters

16. What does Ishmael have tattooed on his forearm?

    A. A naked woman
    B. A spouting whale
    C. The dimensions of a whale
    D. A passage from the Book of Job

17. With what is the Pequod adorned?

    A.   Sperm whale teeth
    B.   American flags
    C.   Red paint
    D.   Whale fins

18. From what is Ahab's false leg made?

    A.   A whale's jawbone
    B.   Wood
    C.   An elephant's tusk
    D.   Leather

19. With which of the following characters does Ishmael share a bed at the Spouter-Inn?

    A.   Starbuck
    B.   Fedallah
    C.   Bildad
    D.   Queequeg

20. Out of what is Fedallah's turban made?

    A.   Whale skin
    B.   His hair
    C.   Silk from China
    D.   Dried seaweed

21. How does the Pequod sink?

    A.   She is rammed by Moby Dick.
    B.   She is overloaded with oil.
    C.   She gets lost in a storm.
    D.   She is rammed by another ship.

22. Who owns the Pequod?

    A.   Father Mapple
    B.   Captain Ahab
    C.   The town of Nantucket
    D.   Bildad and Peleg

23. With what does Queequeg sleep?

    A. The statue of his god
    B. His harpoon
    C. A cat
    D. A bottle of rum

24. Ahab's mates include

    A. Starbuck
    B. Stubb
    C. Flask
    D. All of the above

25. What does Ahab see when he studies the gold doubloon nailed to the mast?

    A. Moby Dick
    B. Himself
    C. God
    D. The face of Evil

Suggestions for Further Reading

BENDER, BERT. *Sea Brothers: The Tradition of American Sea Fiction from* MOBY-DICK *to the Present.* Philadelphia: University of Pennsylvania Press, 1998.

BLOOM, HAROLD, ed. *Herman Melville's* MOBY-DICK. New York: Chelsea House, 1996.

COWAN, BAINARD. *Exiled Waters:* MOBY-DICK *and the Crisis of Allegory.* Baton Rouge: Louisiana State University Press, 1982

DAVEY, MICHAEL. *Herman Melville's* MOBY-DICK: *A Sourcebook.* New York: Routledge, 2003.

HEIMERT, ALAN. MOBY-DICK *and American Political Symbolism.* Cambridge, Massachusetts: The Eliot House Edition, 1991.

LEVINE, ROBERT S., ed. *The Cambridge Companion to Herman Melville.* Cambridge, UK: Cambridge University Press, 1998.

MORRISON, TONI. "Unspeakable Things Unspoken: The Afro-American Presence in American Literature." In *Within the Circle: An Anthology of African American Literary Criticism from the Harlem Renaissance to the Present,* ed. Angelyn Mitchell. Durham, North Carolina: Duke University Press, 1994.

OLSON, CHARLES. *Call Me Ishmael.* Baltimore: Johns Hopkins University Press, 1997.

POST-LAURIA, SHEILA. *Correspondent Colorings: Melville in the Marketplace.* Amherst: University of Massachusetts Press, 1996.

SLADE, LEONARD A. *Symbolism in Herman Melville's* MOBY-DICK: *From the Satanic to the Divine.* Lewiston, New York: E. Mellen Press, 1998.

REVIEW & RESOURCES